Women on the Front Lines

A Call to Courage

Michal Ann Goll

Destiny Image® Publishers, Inc.
P.O. Box 310
Shippensburg, PA 17257-0310

"Speaking to the Purposes of God for This Generation
and for the Generations to Come"

ISBN 0-7684-2020-2

For Worldwide Distribution
Printed in the U.S.A.

6 7 8 9 10 11 12 13 / 10 09 08 07 06 05 04

This book and all other Destiny Image, Revival Press, Mercy Place, Fresh Bread, and Treasure House books are available at Christian bookstores and distributors worldwide.

For a U.S. bookstore nearest you, call **1-800-722-6774**.
For more information on foreign distributors, call **717-532-3040**.
Or reach us on the Internet: **http://www.destinyimage.com**

Dedication

I'd like to dedicate this book to two groups of people. First of all, I dedicate this book to all the dear women from the past—countless numbers of known but mostly unknown courageous saints—who have paid the price of service and true devotion to our Lord. Thank you for passing along to us the baton of faith, hope, and love. Thank you for watching us and cheering us on as we fight our daily battles to win for the Lord the rewards of Christ's suffering. Second, I dedicate this book to all those dear ones who have their future still ahead of them, who are ready and waiting to serve and love the Lord with all their being. May you press forward and be champions for God. Let Him capture your hearts. And give Him everything, for He gave everything for you.

Acknowledgments

First I want to thank my family, for without their love and support I could never have attempted this project. Thank you, dearest Jim, and Justin, GraceAnn, Tyler, and Rachel, for all that you have sacrificed for my sake and for the sake of others.

Thanks also go to the Destiny Image staff for their vision to see women released into the fullness of their destinies and callings in God. Thank you for all your many labors to see this book published.

Our staff at Ministry to the Nations is absolutely the most wonderful, dedicated team there could possibly be. Jim and I count ourselves most fortunate to be working together with these dear friends. Thank you all for your watchful prayers on my behalf, as well as for your practical assistance. Special thanks go to Kathy Colbert, who is my personal assistant.

Dear intercessors, I could not do what I'm doing without you. Thank you for being watchmen on the wall. Thanks go especially to Rick and Annie Stivers, Ann Bell, Dave and Peggy Fitzpatrick,

Pat Gastineau, Sue Kellough, Kelly Rushing, and Bob and Terry Bailey.

I also want to express my thanks to my pastor, Stephen Mansfield, who has provided a place of shelter for me—a covering for women to be pioneers for Christ's Kingdom's sake.

Last, but most important, I want to thank my Lord and King, Jesus Christ, who has opened the door of freedom for me and who cares more about my future than I ever possibly could. I did this book for You, Jesus, and I pray that it will be used to release Your Kingdom life into the lives of many, many men and women.

Endorsements

"I have personally had the joy of knowing Michal Ann Goll for more than 15 years, and I can commend her to you as a 'woman of courage' who longs to see Jesus receive the rewards for His suffering. I give a hearty AMEN to her ministry and the teachings found in this book."

–Mike Bickle
Senior Pastor of Metro Christian Fellowship
Author of *Passion for Jesus*

"Michal Ann, herself, is a woman on the front lines as she becomes more and more courageous with each fresh revelation from her Lord. In my opinion, she stands alongside the nine 'ordinary women' of this book as one who knows an extraordinary God, becoming strong, standing firm, and doing exploits for Him. May the Holy Spirit use this book to open each reader's eyes to see her awesome potential in Him."

–Mary Audrey Raycroft
Pastor of Equipping Ministries and Women in Ministry
Toronto Airport Christian Fellowship
Author of *Releasers of Life*

"While reading *Women on the Front Lines*, my spirit was stirred, motivated, and encouraged to never settle for less than God's purpose and call for my life. This book will take the reader from feeling unimportant and ordinary to realizing that she is God's chosen vessel with a powerful purpose. I believe the Holy Spirit intends us to experience more than mere enjoyment and inspiration from this book's pages; He desires us to receive the invaluable impartation of Michal Ann's zeal and heart to fulfill all of God's mandate."

—Shirley Sustar
Author of *Women of Royalty*

"With a balanced presentation, Michal Ann challenges women to fulfill their potential in God without compromising their femininity. This 'Female Hall of Fame' will inspire our young sisters, who have so few heroes and heroines to look up to as examples."

—Lila Terhune
Intercessory Prayer Coordinator
Brownsville Assembly of God, Pensacola, Florida
Author of *Cross-Pollination*

"Michal Ann Goll is a prophetic intercessor and a radical freedom fighter who has a heart to see women come forth in their destiny. I highly recommend *Women on the Front Lines* as it showcases pioneers and heroines of the faith. It will encourage those women who struggle with intimidation and the fear of man. Her book trumpets a sound of deliverance and mobilization for women in the shadows as well as for those on the front lines to be courageous as they run fervently for their high calling."

—Jill Austin
Conference Speaker and
President of Master Potter Ministries

"This book is intelligent, wise, inspiring, and warm because it flows from the life of Michal Ann Goll. Clearly, this remarkable woman has been chosen to tenderly lead the women of this generation into destined wholeness and Kingdom impact. Michal Ann is one of the women I will tell my daughter to follow as Michal Ann, in turn, follows Jesus. I can give no higher praise."

—Stephen L. Mansfield
Senior Pastor of Belmont Church

Contents

Foreword xiii

Introduction xv

Part I   **Down With Intimidation!** **1**

Chapter 1   No More Fear 3

Chapter 2   I'm in the Army Now! 17

Chapter 3   The Cost of Courage 31

Part II   **Women of Courage** **47**

Chapter 4   Vibia Perpetua: Faithful Unto Death 49

Chapter 5   Sojourner Truth: "Ain't I a Woman?" 59

Chapter 6   Harriet Tubman: Go Down, Moses 71

Chapter 7   Aimee Semple McPherson:
Yesterday, Today, and Forever 81

Chapter 8   Lydia Prince: The Peace of Jerusalem 93

Chapter 9   Bertha Smith: Walking in the Spirit 103

Chapter 10   Corrie ten Boom: No Pit So Deep 115

Chapter 11   Jackie Pullinger-To: Lighting the Darkness .. 127

Part III   **Seize the Day!** **137**

Chapter 12   You Are Chosen! 139

Foreword

As I read the chapters of this wonderful book, my thoughts went back to another woman who struggled with the same issues discussed in these pages—a woman who couldn't pray aloud in a group of 10 or 20; a woman who would rehearse words to prayers that she was never able to pray openly. That woman was me. To this day I marvel as I climb platforms in nations around the world and look into the faces of crowds that sometimes number 20,000 or more.

Women on the Front Lines is full of compassion, exhortation, and encouragement for women who are struggling to become the women of destiny that God has created them to be. Michal Ann has poured out her heart in a vulnerable, even tender way to her fellow sisters in Christ. It is almost as if she is God's cheerleader for the reader, exhorting her with chapters full of, "Go on, Sister, you can do it!" and, "That fear and intimidation don't need to control you!"

God is speaking in a clear voice to His women today, saying, "Women, daughters, handmaidens—it's your time. Rise up. Free yourselves of the bondages that hold you back from your destiny. Don't be content with second best. You are a treasure!"

Woman of God, please read this book. It will change your life.

Cindy Jacobs
Co-Founder of Generals of Intercession

Introduction

Life has many changes and tests of flexibility in it. I know! I remember that night so well. It was about the fifth week of visitations from God in our home in the fall of 1992 when Michal Ann and I had our pivotal, now famous conversation. With the fear of God on me I stated, "I don't know who you are or who you are becoming!" She responded with an equal dose of intensity, "I don't know who I am or who I am becoming either!" I know this may be hard to comprehend, but we both sighed with relief and knew that at least we were still in agreement, still very much in the Lord's hands, and could continue on this revolutionary journey of "becoming all that He has intended us to be."

What does this have to do with this book, you say? Everything! My wife's life changed! *Our* lives changed! And we continue to be challenged and changed. Now I want to see this same God of change come and "rock your boat," deliver you from the shackles of fear and intimidation, and infuse you with this same spirit of courage and might that so powerfully impacted my wife in those days. Yes, Michal Ann and I want you to become all that He wants you to be in Jesus' name! That's what this challenging book is all about—the contagious change through the empowering work of the Holy Spirit that is called courage!

If that is what you want, if that is what you hunger and thirst for, then dear reader, this book was penned with you in mind. Let me give you a brief overview of what to expect in this inspiring book, *Women on the Front Lines: A Call to Courage.*

Part One, "Down With Intimidation!" tells of the personal journey my wife has been on in her walk with the Lord. This first part is extremely relatable, filled with true-to-life stories from an authentic, normal, everyday woman of God. The first part closes out with Michal Ann's inspirational look at the life of Joan of Arc, whose story has so dramatically impacted her own life in recent years.

Part Two, "Women of Courage," takes a journey through Church history up unto today and showcases examples of women used by God on the front lines. Consider these women: Perpetua, a martyr for her faith in the early Church; Sojourner Truth, a black woman leader in the anti-slavery movement; and Harriet Tubman, another dedicated black pioneer of the Underground Railroad to freedom in the time before the Civil War. Consider the inspiration from the life of Aimee Semple McPherson, a woman healing evangelist at the turn of the twentieth century; Lydia Christensen-Prince, forerunner for the cause of orphans and the purposes of God among the Jewish people; and Bertha Smith, a Baptist woman missionary and revival leader in Shantung, China. Then we glance at the wondrous life of Corrie ten Boom as she suffered for the cause of Christ and the Jewish people in the time of the Holocaust; and lastly, we shine a light on a courageous woman of this generation: Jackie Pullinger-To, a British evangelist and missionary in the Walled City of Hong Kong. Awesome! Yes, women of courage have been mightily used throughout the pages of Church history.

The third and last part of *Women on the Front Lines*, "Seize the Day!" takes us back to some inspiring lessons of courage from my dear wife's life and teaching that the Lord has given to her. But please hear this! This is not a "sexist book." This is more than a women's testimonial novel. The truths in this book apply to each one of us—whether we are men or women, old or young! These are lessons learned in the trenches of authentic Christianity about the power of the Holy Spirit to enable each one of us to be more than a conqueror through Christ Jesus, our Master and Lord.

Yes, I recommend this book to each of you. Do you want to know why? It's not just because I believe in the lady who birthed it—which of course I do. But I recommend it because it's relatable. It's got true grit. It's about the lives of ordinary women changed by their consuming God into vessels of honor and courage for their generation and time. May the impact of this book, *Women on the Front Lines: A Call to Courage*, be as challenging and inspiring as those weeks of visitation were to us in the fall of 1992. Go, Holy Spirit; overwhelm these readers and make them into radical, courageous, God-fearing Christians for the honor of Your great name!

Jim W. Goll
Author of *The Lost Art of Intercession*
Co-Founder of Ministry to the Nations
Antioch, Tennessee

Part I

Down With Intimidation!

Chapter 1

*No More Fear**

"Don't let your fears stand in the way of your dreams."

Does that statement speak to you? It sure spoke to me the first time I read it several years ago. I have always been by nature a very quiet and reserved person. But until a few years ago I was also tied up by fear and intimidation, and I hated it. There was so much in me that wanted to come out, but I felt tied down inside. I was like a runner who longed to run but couldn't because heavy chains and weights hung on her ankles, holding her back. Sometimes I wanted to just reach out to someone who was hurting and give her a hug or an encouraging word—just simple things—but I couldn't. I wasn't able to step out beyond myself. For years I cried out, "Lord, I want to be totally sold out to You. I want to be so consumed with You that my fear is completely annihilated." God answered my prayer, granting me the grace to walk in places where I had never walked before.

---

* For a more in-depth study of Michal Ann's encounters with the Lord in this area, refer to Jim and Michal Ann Goll's book, *Encounters With a Supernatural God.*

It all started several years ago when my husband Jim and I were leading a retreat in Nashville, Tennessee. While there I found myself particularly preoccupied with this whole issue of fear and intimidation. In my heart I wanted so badly to be free. It weighed heavily on my mind, eating away at me on the inside.

On the Sunday morning of the retreat I was feeling a strong intercessory burden from the Lord for the people there and was crying out to Him on their behalf. Many of them were in situations where they had little room to function; they had no real opportunity for service or ministry. They felt bottled up, as if they were all crowding together trying to get a whiff of the tiny amount of oxygen that was coming through the narrow neck of the bottle.

In the middle of this intercession, two ladies, dear friends of mine, came up to me and asked if they could pray for me. We went into a little side room and immediately they began spiritual warfare over me, coming against the spirit of intimidation. As soon as they started praying I let out a loud scream. Not very long after that, someone came to the door and said that we were too noisy. The group in the other room had gotten very quiet because they were observing communion. I wanted to be sensitive to what was going on in there, but I also was afraid that if I held back at that point, I would never get free. It was as though the Lord was challenging me, "How badly do you want to be delivered from this thing?"

My friends kept praying and I kept yelling until all of a sudden it was as though something literally lifted right out of the top of my head, leaving an empty space. The best way I can describe it is that this thing felt like a railroad spike: six inches long and about two inches in diameter at the top, tapering to a point at the bottom. It was the strangest sensation. I've never felt anything else like it either before or since. I knew something had happened in me, but at first I didn't really know what it was.

The retreat ended and the people went home, but Jim and I stayed. We had decided to remain at the retreat center overnight so that we could have some time alone. Later that day we went for a walk. With the meetings over, Jim was in a relaxed, silly mood while I was still in a contemplative frame of mind, trying to figure out what God had done with me and what I was supposed to do now. As we walked along Jim was playfully clapping his hands and hitting me on the shoulder. I didn't really want that at that moment. He was invading my "personal space." So I said as nicely as I could, "Jim, please don't do that."

"Don't do what?"

"Please don't hit me."

"Hey, I'm not hitting you," Jim teased as he kept whapping my shoulder.

After I appealed to him again he turned to me, rolled up his sleeve, and said, "Okay, you hit me."

I looked at his arm and, seeing what a good target it was, doubled up my fist and popped him good. I didn't really hit him very hard, but the fact that I did it at all shocked both of us. I had never hit anyone in my life! The expression on Jim's face said, "I can't believe you did that!" My jaw dropped too: "I can't believe I did that!" Then we both started laughing. We realized at that moment that what my friends had prayed for had happened: God had truly delivered me from intimidation.

To intimidate means to make someone timid or fearful; it is to frighten them with threats. At one time the enemy's threats had made me timid; I lacked courage, self-confidence, boldness, and determination. He had filled my mind with fearful thoughts: "If you try this, you are going to fail. You're going to fall flat on your face. You will be misunderstood and all alone." Sometimes panic welled up inside as I found myself saying, "I can't do this! I'm not smart enough, not spiritual enough. I know I'm going to fail!" For a long time I lacked the courage and boldness I needed to press on through.

Once God delivered me, however, it was as though He had attached jumper cables to my spiritual battery! The life and energy of the blood of Jesus flooded my being and set me free! The fear of man was gone—that anxious dread and concern about what other people would think or say about me. Now I could enter into a fuller dimension of the fear of the Lord. The fear of man had filled me with shame and panic; the fear of the Lord filled me with profound reverence and awe toward God. The fear of the Lord is clean, enduring forever. It brings my sins into the light, not to shame or embarrass me, but to cleanse me, forgive me, and justify me, just as if I had never sinned!

I still struggle with intimidation on occasion. Although it is no longer in me, it tries to come against me from time to time, and I have to be alert and ready to deal with it. Intimidation is a spirit, and many Christians, both men and women, are bound by it. God wants us all to be free, not just for the sake of freedom, but so we can truly commune with Him face to face. He wants to take us to a place where we can walk with Him, full of the fear of the Lord, where the fear of man is completely gone. He wants to deliver us from intimidation and its companion spirits of comparison, shame, guilt, and the fear of man. He wants us to be able to fulfill our destiny, to complete our calling in Him, to do those things that each of us is uniquely qualified and designed to accomplish!

Fearless and Free

God seeks and desires a personal relationship with each and every one of us, and He is jealous about that relationship. He is fighting on our behalf to set us free from the cloaks of fear, intimidation, and comparison that the enemy uses to try to smother the life-breath out of us.

I was raised in a devout Methodist family. My grandmother was a sweet, wonderful woman who loved God. Even when she was suffering from cancer she always challenged me and my cousins to put Jesus first in our lives. I cherish that rich heritage from which

I received a deep deposit of the Word of God. However, I did not understand the ways of the Spirit. For a long time after I married Jim I tried to hang on to his coattails; I simply followed what he was doing. Unknowingly, I was comparing my walk with God to Jim's walk, thinking that his was better than mine. God did not see it that way, and He told me so. One day the Lord said to me, "Ann, you can't hold on to Jim's coattails; hold on to Mine. I am your God! I created you, and I am jealous over you. I won't settle for a relationship through your husband; I want a relationship with you." He desires the same for each of us. We cannot relate to Him through anyone else: spouse, pastor, parents, friends, or anyone! Our God is a personal God!

We are His beloved and we are beautiful in His eyes. He sees us through the precious blood of Jesus, His Son. He doesn't see our faults; rather, He sees only Jesus' righteousness covering us. Instead of sin, He sees the beauty of a forgiven soul. We are beautiful to Him when we're sweating, or when we're lying on the floor in deep travail, or when we're crying with runny noses because God is touching a hurting heart. We are beautiful to Him whether we're shaking, trembling, or jumping. We are beautiful to Him when we are at home with our hearts breaking and we think no one knows or cares.

God looks for the beauty of the heart. I believe that any time we bring life into the world or into some needy soul is a time of unparalleled beauty in God's eyes. God loves life! Consider for a moment the appearance and condition of a woman in childbirth: vulnerable, painful, difficult. Most of us who have been through it don't want to be reminded of our appearance! God, however, tells us to look at the heart of the issue.

Our approval from God doesn't depend on whether or not our fingernails are polished, our hair is combed, or our houses are neat and tidy with everything in order. God looks at the heart. He created each of us as unique individuals with a fragrance all our own, and He waits in longing to smell that fragrance rising to Him.

He loves us and fashioned us to be creative according to how He has gifted us.

Let God release you to be who He made you to be: a creative individual free from intimidation and the fear of man. Have you ever found yourself at a buffet and, as you pick up your plate to go through the line, you check to see how much food everyone else is taking, then take the same amount? You don't want to take "too much." After all, you have to be careful how you present yourself, right? That's intimidation speaking! I've got good news for you: God has a buffet all laid out, and He wants you to take the biggest plate you can find and load it up. He wants you to pull your chair right up to the table and dig in because the table is spread for you. There are all kinds of breads, pastries, salads and vegetables, luscious fruits, scrumptious desserts; wow, what a feast!

Exposing the Enemy

Let's cast the light of God's Word into the darkness surrounding this issue and expose the enemy. The Lord wants all His children to be free. In these days He is especially trumpeting the deliverance call for His daughters to walk in freedom and to live without fear. God has given His Spirit to His children to help them obtain this freedom. Paul wrote to the Corinthians, "Now the Lord is the Spirit, and where the Spirit of the Lord is, there is liberty (emancipation from bondage, freedom)" (2 Cor. 3:17). The Holy Spirit in us does not produce fear, but power: "For God did not give us a spirit of timidity (of cowardice, of craven and cringing and fawning fear), but [He has given us a spirit] of power and of love and of calm and well-balanced mind and discipline and self-control" (2 Tim. 1:7). His goal is to produce in us a full and perfect love that eliminates and replaces fear.

There is no fear in love [dread does not exist], but full-grown (complete, perfect) love turns fear out of doors and expels every trace of terror! For fear brings with it the thought of punishment,

8

and [so] he who is afraid has not reached the full maturity of love
[is not yet grown into love's complete perfection] (1 John 4:18).

Favored and Forgiven

According to Esther 2:9, the young Jewish maiden Esther, who was destined to be the queen of King Xerxes, found favor in the eyes of Hegai. Now Hegai was the eunuch in charge of the king's harem. He gave Esther seven personal maidservants and moved all of them into the most favored place in the harem. That is favor! In the same way, God has given us, His daughters, the most favored place. Unfortunately, many of us as women struggle with thoughts or feelings of unworthiness and low self-esteem. Some have trouble trusting men because men have stepped on them and held them back. God wants to heal all that. He wants to reprogram our thinking. He wants to remove the intimidation as well as the spirit of comparison that makes us think that we can't do anything until we first become like somebody else. I believe God is saying to us, "Be yourself. I created you, and I love you just the way you are."

What about the past? All of us have painful memories of sins or mistakes that we have made. One of satan's most powerful weapons is to bring those past things before us and beat us over the head with them. Too many times we help him out by listening to his accusations and agreeing with him. As a result, guilt, shame, fear, and intimidation rise up and tie us down, holding us back from all that God wants to do in us.

Don't be bound by the mistakes of the past. Don't allow them to keep rising up, or they will keep you from stepping out for fear of failure. There is complete freedom and release in God's forgiveness. John, the beloved apostle, wrote:

If we [freely] admit that we have sinned and confess our sins, He
is faithful and just (true to His own nature and promises) and will
forgive our sins [dismiss our lawlessness] and [continuously]

cleanse us from all unrighteousness [everything not in conformity to His will in purpose, thought, and action] (1 John 1:9).

Whatever God forgives, He forgets. He says in Isaiah, "I, even I, am He Who blots out and cancels your transgressions, for My own sake, and I will not remember your sins" (Is. 43:25). King David reminds us that, "As far as the east is from the west, so far has He removed our transgressions from us" (Ps. 103:12). When we confess our sins, God forgives them and then forgets them. He remembers our sins no more, and we stand clean and pure before Him.

He wants to woo us, to draw us into His holy presence. When we come into that place, all fear simply drops away. We walk unashamed with our heads lifted high, our eyes meeting His eyes, like a bride approaching her bridegroom. No shame, no embarrassment, no fear, no intimidation—all are cast out by the power of His captivating and all-consuming love. The sound of His voice delights us as we hear Him say, "Oh, how I've waited for you to come! How I've longed to embrace you, to be with you, to be in union with you." His love goes far beyond what we can possibly ask, think, or imagine (see Eph. 3:20).

Visitations in the Night

There was a time when I got quite jealous of my husband. Jim would go off to different conferences and meetings and such, and I would be at home with the children. He would come back all pumped up and excited over what the Lord had done, while I had spent the weekend with dirty diapers and a house that showed all the symptoms of four small children. In addition, I was home-schooling our oldest child and our family was in the midst of a major move. Jim was getting all these neat blessings from God and I was missing out. I simply had no time for anything.

One day, out of despair and frustration, I leaned against the wall and said, "Lord, I want so much to be with You, but I am so busy. I just don't have the time to sit and soak in Your presence.

No More Fear

From the time I get up in the morning until I go to bed at night, my time is not my own. Even at night my kids wake up, and I have to be there."

The Lord answered me so sweetly and gently. He said, "Ann, I know all that. I am the God of the impossible, and what you think is impossible is possible with Me. I will come to you. I will visit you in the night."

Shortly after that, He began speaking to me in dreams, totally rearranging my perception of both myself and Him. He showed me how He could use me as I gave Him complete control of my life. He showed me how much He loved me and longed for fellowship with me. For example, I had one dream in which God was represented by an older gentleman whom I could sense loved me deeply. He loved the fragrance of my hair and yearned for me to reach out and hug Him. He could hardly wait for me to embrace Him so that He could smell my hair. I had never, ever imagined that anyone could love me that way, but that's the way God loves us!

During this time of visitation, the Lord gave me a dream that dealt with this whole issue of intimidation—how strong of a force it can be and how it can tempt us to do things that we would not otherwise do. In this dream, my oldest son Justin and I were in China running food, clothing, and other items to needy people. We had to be very careful, moving quickly from place to place so that the enemy would not catch us.

As I was preparing to leave one house, the authorities broke in and grabbed me. Justin had already left, so he escaped. I, however, was taken into the yard to face the enemy leader. He wanted to punish me by torture—hanging me by the neck, not until I died, but long enough to choke me and leave rope marks on my neck. There were several other prisoners in the yard who had already been punished this way. It was a very intimidating situation. I was thinking, *He doesn't want to kill me; just hang me for a little while. That's not so bad!*

11

I almost consented to the punishment when all of a sudden a light went on inside me. *How foolish of me to entrust my life into the enemy's hands!* Once the noose was around my neck, I would be completely at his mercy. How could I trust the word of the enemy?

In the dream, rather than giving in to the intimidation and agreeing to the punishment, I began preaching the gospel to the enemy leader. He was intrigued and let me continue, leading me and the other prisoners into his court chamber where there were approximately 50 chairs around a huge oval-shaped table. There was another table and a row of chairs on an elevated platform at one end of the room. Both the room and the furniture were dark. As I continued preaching the Word to this enemy leader, I felt like Paul preaching to King Agrippa. I pulled from my pocket an uncut, unpolished purple gem, like an amethyst. As I spoke, the gem grew larger and larger and became brighter and brighter. The enemy leader reached out to take the stone in his hand. It continued to grow as I continued to preach the Word. He was holding a miracle, a wonder of God in his own hand, and with his own eyes watched it grow and glow.

It seems to me that the gem in this dream symbolizes the Word coming forth from within. When we are on the verge of a breakthrough, the enemy will come and try to intimidate us and make us settle for something less than we should. If we press through and confront the enemy of intimidation, though, allowing the boldness of the Holy Spirit to come on us, we become like the stone, growing and glowing with the truth and power of God's Word.

We are all choice and precious stones, and we must stir up the gifting and the calling that are within us. If we allow intimidation to take over, it will choke us. We cannot speak with nooses around our necks. When we let the boldness of the Lord come out, however, those uncut gems in us glow and grow—a visible miracle to the world.

No More Fear

The time has come for us to do business with God and with the enemy. It's time to decide to not let intimidation and fear strangle us any longer; to not give our lives to the enemy, trusting him to hurt us only a little. God has set the day of deliverance! It's time for us to take the nooses off, bring the gems out of our pockets, and witness the miracle that God wants to do in us.

Building Bridges

Do you find it easier to believe that God will do something for someone else than to believe that He will do something for you? Do you find it difficult to accept the possibility that God could really use you, that He can take you out of your shell and remove all fear from your heart? God is no respecter of persons, and if He did it for me, He will do it for you.

Not long ago I was on a plane and was settling in my seat to read a book during the flight. As it happened, it was a book about how to deal with intimidation, and I was on my way to a conference to speak on that very subject. I was in an aisle seat. Very soon I became uncomfortably aware of a man in the aisle seat across from me staring at me. I found myself thinking, *Am I going to have to walk through this issue of intimidation even before I get up and talk about it?*

So I sat there with this man staring at me the whole time, and I was telling myself over and over, *I will not be intimidated....I will not be intimidated....I will not be intimidated....*while I sat there trying to read my book and my Bible. This continued for the entire flight, which was a little over an hour.

Finally, as we were preparing to land, he leaned over and asked, "What synagogue do you go to?"

At first I did not understand what he meant. Then I realized that he had seen the Star of David I was wearing. It is a symbol of my love and burden for the Jews and for the nation of Israel.

13

I said to him, "Oh, I'm a Christian, but I love the Jews." I think I totally confused him. He did not know what to do. Here he had sat on the plane for over an hour trying to figure out how to ask me that question; and when he finally did, my answer baffled him.

I mention this incident because as we learn to deal with fear and intimidation, we will find that God will bring circumstances across our paths that may intimidate us or make us fearful, when actually God just wants to use us. We have to get out of our comfort zones and open our hearts and mouths for God's sake. As God uses us to draw people to Him, people will begin looking at us and talking with us. We have to learn to not be fearful when that happens. Instead, we need to recognize both the hand of God as He moves in that other person's life and the part we are to play in what He is doing.

We need to change our "stinking thinking." Up with the positive, down with the negative! It's time for divine appointments. God wants to do so much through us, but we have to get rid of our fear. For example, He wants to release in us new ways of evangelism that we have not even dreamed of. We have become so bound up in our minds by traditional ideas of what evangelism looks like and how it should be done that God has trouble getting through to us. He is saying, "I have all kinds of creative ways and ideas that I want to release, but you've got to get rid of your fear."

I've heard it said that the word F-E-A-R stands for "False Evidence Appearing Real." The devil is a liar and a thief; he will steal us blind if we let him. God speaks the truth! It is vital to our life in Him that we reject all the lies the devil has fed us and step out in faith into what God says. We must get into the Bible, studying it and reading for ourselves God's promises toward us. It is only by knowing the goodness and faithfulness of God and by applying the power of the blood and name of Jesus in our lives that we can dislodge and decimate satan's plans.

No More Fear

We've got to be free to see, but we can't see if we're bound up in fear. Have you ever been introduced to someone and not caught his or her name because you were so concerned about what you were going to say in response? That's intimidation. Once you are free of it, you can look at someone and think about that person rather than worrying about yourself. In that way you can be God's hands and God's voice to people and build bridges of love, not fear.

Getting rid of fear and intimidation means getting out of yourself and into Christ; moving from concern over how you look or what you are going to say to asking, "Lord, what do You have for this person?" It is when you get out of yourself that you become truly free. Learning to be free is a lifelong process; but in Christ you have everything you need, and it is never too late to begin.

Dare to Dream

Several years ago I was scheduled to speak at a women's conference in Kansas City on the theme, "Overcoming Intimidation." At that time I had not spoken at many conferences and still felt insecure about doing them. I knew that I had to conquer the enemy of intimidation that was coming against me if I was to succeed at this conference. I felt like I needed a lot of prayer time in order to prepare, but the only "quiet" times I had came in 15-minute segments while I drove back and forth between home and the school. On the Friday that the conference began, just a few hours before the first meeting, my final, desperate prayer was, "God, let me do this with no fear!"

As soon as I uttered the words I saw a picture in my mind of me wearing a T-shirt with the words "No Fear" across the front. I said to God, "All right, as I speak on Saturday morning I will envision 'No Fear' written across my heart, guarding me. In faith I will believe that You will accomplish this!"

When I told Jim about it later that evening, he insisted that I had to get a "No Fear" T-shirt and wear it. I had no time for shopping though, so he did it for me while I was at the Friday night meeting. I returned home to find laid out on the kitchen counter two T-shirts and two hats with "No Fear" on the front. One set was for me; the other was for Jim. In addition, inside the rim of my hat were the words that opened this chapter: "Don't let your fears stand in the way of your dreams."

Here was yet another testimony to God's faithfulness and to the personal, individual care He gives to each of us. After years of trying to deal with my fears and after many, many dreams through which God had given me hope, the time had come for me to apply what I had been learning. God was saying to me, "Gird your mind with the dreams I have placed in you and go, girl!"

I want to issue this challenge to you: *Dare to dream!* Open up your heart in a fresh way and ask God to put a dream there. Ask Him to dust off the promise book with your name on it and make those promises real and fresh to you!

Don't let your fears stand in the way of your dreams! Take out the spike of intimidation and, like the Israelite woman Jael did to the Philistine Sisera in Judges 4, drive it into the enemy's head and kill the plans and schemes he has devised against you. We must be ruthless with the devil; he surely has no mercy on us!

Chapter 2

I'm in the Army Now!

Any army that hopes to achieve victory in battle must have disciplined and well-trained soldiers, dependable supply lines, and a clear strategy. If any of these elements are weak or lacking, the chances of success decrease drastically. In the same way, before we as soldiers of the Lord can successfully engage in battle with an enemy as ruthless and merciless as the devil, we must become well-trained, well-equipped disciples committed to carrying out our Commander's plan of action.

We are individual soldiers joined together in a great army called the Church, and we are commissioned to do battle "against the despotisms, against the powers, against [the master spirits who are] the world rulers of this present darkness, against the spirit forces of wickedness in the heavenly (supernatural) sphere" (Eph. 6:12b). Victory depends on all of us working together in obedience to our Lord and not trying to move out on our own. None of us by ourselves is a match for the enemy. In fact, any believer, no matter who it is, who tries to take on the devil alone embarks on a suicide mission.

When Jesus established His Church, He promised that the gates of hell would not prevail against it (see Mt. 16:18). His promise is for the *Church*—individual believers working together in unity and harmony to fulfill Jesus' commission to make disciples of all the nations. Just as soldiers are trained to do specific jobs in conjunction with others to achieve the overall mission, so each of us must find our place and operate in our gifts in conjunction with each other in order to accomplish our mission as Christ's army, the Church.

Annie, Get Your Gun

Years ago God spoke to me in a dream about the importance of being thoroughly prepared to do battle with the enemy. The images were so vivid and intense that they have remained with me ever since. In my dream I was inside the comfortable old farmhouse of my childhood. Normally full of warmth, charm, family love, and belonging, the house was now a place of fear and panic. I was alone and in an upstairs bedroom, and an intruder had entered the house.

Spread out on the bed before me were several handguns of different styles and calibers, along with bullets for each of them. The intruder began coming up the stairs. My mind screamed, *Which one?! Which one?!* as I fumbled with the weapons, trying frantically to figure out which bullets went with which gun so that I could load one of them and use it to defend myself. Before I could do so, the bedroom door burst open and the intruder entered, pointing a gun at me. Rushing over to the bed, he quickly overpowered me and dragged me to the floor. Then he was on top of me, and I was fighting desperately to get him off.

My dream ended at that point, leaving me with a terrible ache in my heart. I realized that I did not know the weapons of my warfare. Oh, I knew that I had some, but I wasn't familiar enough with them to use them effectively. I didn't even know which bullet went with which gun, much less have any of the guns loaded and ready. How could I possibly be prepared for attacks from the enemy?

I'm in the Army Now!

I couldn't very well say to him, "Wait a minute! You can't come after me yet. I have to load my gun!"

This started me on a major quest of asking the Lord, "Please, God, show me what my spiritual weapons are and how to use them. Help me to be ready to use them against the enemy whenever he comes against me." I needed to be a trick shooter like Annie Oakley, as skilled with my weapons as she was with hers!

Courage on the front lines of faith requires a thorough knowledge of the spiritual weapons and other resources that we have, as well as supreme devotion to and confidence in the One for whom we fight and who fights for us, taking our battles upon Himself. We can be encouraged in the assurance that God's banner is over us, His blessings are upon us, and His boldness is in us.

God's Banner Over Us

It is written in the Song of Solomon, "He brought me to the banqueting house, and his banner over me was love [for love waved as a protecting and comforting banner over my head when I was near him]" (Song 2:4). God has stretched this great protective banner of His love over our heads. As we look up we can see written on it the words, "God is faithful, God is true." Yet the words are hard to make out because we who are believers have covered them with a film of unbelief and doubt that clouds them from our vision. Whenever anything negative comes along, our enemy infiltrates our thoughts and eats away at our confidence in God, of how much He loves us and cares for us. We begin to see holes here and there in the banner; the film gets darker, the words harder to see.

All of us go through bad experiences from time to time; and if we are not careful, satan uses them to eat away at our faith. Maybe you try to move in something that you believe God wants you to do. You step out like Peter, climbing out of the boat to walk to Jesus, but something goes wrong and you sink. All of a sudden the banner over your head that says, "God is faithful," has a chunk out of it. You are left thinking, *Well, God is faithful, but maybe He's not as faithful with me as He is with someone else.* The seeds of doubt begin to grow.

Perhaps you are praying faithfully and fervently for someone's healing and don't understand when that person dies and goes to be with the Lord. Another hole appears in the banner and you think, *Well, if God is faithful, why does He heal sometimes but not at others?* Such questions enter our minds, are written on our hearts, and block us from fully believing that God truly is faithful and that He really will do everything that He said He will do.

This process can reach the point where we believe that God will move in somebody else's life but not in ours. He will work in their church but not in ours; He will come through for them but not for us. There are just enough negative experiences for us to wonder about God. Is God faithful? Can we trust Him to be true to His Word?

King David wrote, "Your mercy and loving-kindness, O Lord, extend to the skies, and Your faithfulness to the clouds" (Ps. 36:5). Psalm 100 affirms, "For the Lord is good; His mercy and loving-kindness are everlasting, His faithfulness and truth endure to all generations" (Ps. 100:5). The prophet Isaiah proclaimed, "O Lord, You are my God; I will exalt You, I will praise Your name, for You have done wonderful things, even purposes planned of old [and fulfilled] in faithfulness and truth" (Is. 25:1). The Book of Lamentations says, "It is because of the Lord's mercy and loving-kindness that we are not consumed, because His [tender] compassions fail not. They are new every morning; great and abundant is Your stability and faithfulness" (Lam. 3:22-23).

Yes, God *is* faithful! Yes, you can trust Him to be true to His Word. The Lord wants to really shine down on you. He wants for you simply to believe Him. It's time for you to settle this issue once and for all. It's time to remove the questions from your mind and the doubts from your heart and to acknowledge to God, "Lord, I have fallen for the enemy's lies. He has come in and chipped away little pieces out of me and out of my faith in You. Forgive me, Lord. Please restore to me all those things that he has taken. Give me the faith and courage to step out and remove the dark film from the banner, to boldly reclaim Your promise that says, 'God is faithful.'"

The Heavens Declare God's Faithfulness

In fact, like Solomon's banner, God's faithfulness is written in the skies above us. Psalm 89 says, "For I have said, Mercy and loving-kindness shall be built up forever; Your faithfulness will You establish in the very heavens [unchangeable and perpetual]" (Ps. 89:2).

When our oldest son Justin was in the sixth grade, all the students in his grade gave a presentation on the constellations for all the parents and teachers. Each student took one constellation, made a large replica of it, and identified by name the different stars that made up the constellation. These are ancient names; some of them go back 5,000 years. Each student also researched the meanings of these ancient names.

I was a little unsure about it at first. When I heard the word *constellation*, I tended to think of astrology and the zodiac and everything associated with them. So I was a little uneasy until I realized that satan had taken what the Lord placed in the heavens as signs of His faithfulness, and twisted and distorted them until we will barely look at them, much less see God's handiwork in them.

The presentation was wonderful. It was incredible to see all the pictures and hear about the meanings behind the stars' names and the constellations themselves. All of it was a reminder of God's loving kindness and mercy displayed in the heavens themselves. Some of these were pictures of sheep coming into the sheepfold, and of Jesus the great Shepherd guarding the sheepfold and protecting them. One was about Jesus, the strong and mighty warrior, with

His boots on, crushing the head of the serpent underneath His feet. Later, I told Justin's teacher how impressed I was with the whole thing. It was awesome just hearing about God's loving-kindness being displayed in the heavenlies, day after day, year after year.

Those stars are millions and billions of miles away. Some are closer to us than others, yet God has arranged them in such a way that from our perspective we see shapes, sometimes almost as clearly as if they were pictures hanging on a wall. The constellations are a constant reminder to us of God's faithfulness. Like a heavenly banner, He set the stars in place to remind us, generation after generation after generation, of His faithfulness.

God wants to restore His banner of love and faithfulness over each of us individually, but there is also a cry in His heart for it to be stretched out to cover everyone. He wants us to stretch it out over our families, our churches, and our communities so that we are no longer saying only, "God is faithful to me," but "God is faithful to my family, my church, and my city." As we proclaim God's faithfulness and the banner spreads, and as everybody takes their banner, all of a sudden the banners interlace together as one large sheltering canopy. That releases the Lord to do more, because by it we are affirming our belief in Him and in His faithfulness. God has said that His banner over us is love and that He is faithful, and God is always true to His Word.

God's Blessings Upon Us

Courage for faithful service on the front lines also comes in the knowledge that the Lord does not send us out on our own. His presence is always with us, and His blessings are upon us to especially equip us for the work He has called us to do. In Psalm 103 King David provides a wonderfully encouraging list of blessings that God has given to His children. Appropriately, David begins the psalm with praise:

I'm in the Army Now!

Bless (affectionately, gratefully praise) the Lord, O my soul; and all that is [deepest] within me, bless His holy name! Bless (affectionately, gratefully praise) the Lord, O my soul, and forget not [one of] all His benefits (Psalm 103:1-2).

David calls the blessings of God, "His benefits." That makes me think of an insurance salesman sitting down at the table and saying, "Okay, now let me show you all the benefits you will receive if you sign up for our policy." God provides many benefits.

"Who forgives [every one of] all your iniquities..." (Ps. 103:3a). God forgives all our iniquities—all the mistakes, all the stubbornness, all the pride. He forgives our attempts to control Him and others. Whatever our sin, if we confess it to Him, He forgives it. Whatever God forgives, He forgets. It is as if we were to hand God a piece of paper with all our sins written on it (it would be a long piece of paper!) and say, "Lord, here are my sins. Please forgive me." He would return the paper to us not with the sins checked or even scratched out, but with them completely gone! The paper would be perfectly white without wrinkle or mark; it would be fresh, clean, and new. God's forgiveness makes it as though we had never sinned. His forgiveness removes sin-guilt as a weapon for satan to use against us. God is faithful.

"Who heals [each one of] all your diseases" (Ps. 103:3b). God is our healer; He heals all our diseases. Now I don't understand why some people don't get healed, but I do know that God is faithful and that He has great compassion for His children.

My mother died of cancer in 1982. Before she died, I really expected God to heal her. When He didn't, I had some questions at first about His faithfulness. Mom was a Christian, so I knew that she was with Jesus. After she died, I had many dreams of her in Heaven happy and at peace, a new creation with her flesh restored, and I knew that she was much better off being with the Lord. My questions subsided. Once again, God had proven His faithfulness.

There have been times, I confess, when I have felt cheated at not having my mom. She and I were just becoming really good friends and were growing very close at the time of her death. She also never got to meet any of her grandchildren, although she believed that someone in the family was pregnant. As it turned out, I was carrying our first child, Justin, but didn't find out until after Mom died. Justin's birth was a great balm to my soul, coming as it did so soon after Mom's death and after eight years of barrenness. In the midst of it all, God showed once more that He is faithful.

"*Who redeems your life from the pit and corruption, Who beautifies, dignifies, and crowns you with loving-kindness and tender mercy*" (Ps. 103:4). Isn't that beautiful? Think of the transformation: Jesus lifted us from the slime, dirt, mud, and refuse of the pit. He cleaned us up, giving us new clothes and a crown engraved with the words, "loving-kindness and tender mercy." He placed us on the rock to reign with Him.

"*Who satisfies your mouth [your necessity and desire at your personal age and situation] with good so that your youth, renewed, is like the eagle's [strong, overcoming, soaring]! The Lord executes righteousness and justice [not for me only, but] for all who are oppressed*" (Ps. 103:5-6). God knows just how to meet our needs, whatever our age or situation. His presence and provision always renew our strength so that we can fly! Whenever we are oppressed by our employer or a fellow worker, or under pressure anywhere else, we can trust that God is faithful to see our need and respond in righteousness and justice.

"*He made known His ways [of righteousness and justice] to Moses, His acts to the children of Israel. The Lord is merciful and gracious, slow to anger and plenteous in mercy and loving-kindness. He will not always chide or be contending, neither will He keep His anger forever or hold a grudge*" (Ps. 103:7-9). How many times have you tried and failed repeatedly at something until you felt that the Lord would be really mad at you if you failed again? Repeated failure can bring discouragement. Maybe you remember a time when you really messed things up and your mistake affected the lives of a lot of people. Doesn't the Lord remember too and hold it against you? No way! He is merciful, gracious, slow to anger, and never holds a grudge. Those negative thoughts are attacks from the enemy. Shoot them down with the weapons of God's faithfulness, mercy, and loving-kindness.

The depth of God's love, mercy, and blessings toward us is brought out in the next several verses of the psalm:

> *He has not dealt with us after our sins nor rewarded us according to our iniquities. For as the heavens are high above the earth, so great are His mercy and loving-kindness toward those who reverently and worshipfully fear Him. As far as the east is from the west, so far has He removed our transgressions from us. As a father loves and pities His children, so the Lord loves and pities those who fear Him [with reverence, worship, and awe]. For He knows our frame, He [earnestly] remembers and imprints [on His heart] that we are dust* (Psalm 103:10-14).

Isn't it wonderful that God hasn't given us the judgment that our sins deserve, but has instead poured out His mercy on us? What confidence we can have in Christ when we know that our sins have been removed from us "as far as the east is from the west"! God blesses us and supports us because He knows how weak we are and how much in need we are; He knows that we cannot last on our own. Both the confidence that our sins are forgiven and the presence of the Holy Spirit in us give us a holy boldness as we serve on the front lines of faith.

God's Boldness in Us

In Acts 4 the Church in Jerusalem, after hearing a report from Peter and John regarding the threats they had received from the chief priests for preaching the gospel, came together and prayed for boldness in the face of opposition. Acts 4:31 says that after their prayer, the place where they were meeting was shaken. They were all filled with the Holy Spirit and proclaimed Christ with courage and boldness. It was because of this divine boldness and power that the early Church was so effective in spreading the gospel throughout the world of its day. God provides that same boldness and courage to us today to spread the gospel throughout our world.

God's Courage

Unfortunately many believers have the wrong concept of courage. The enemy has fed us a lie that says courage means being without fear. This lie says that if we struggle with fear, then we are not courageous people. That is absolutely not true. All of us, even the most courageous among us, have to deal with fears. Courage does not mean having no fear. On the contrary, courage means acknowledging our fear, turning it over to God, and pressing ahead in spite of it. Courage means regarding the dream as more powerful and worthwhile than the fear that would keep us from it.

Courage arises out of the security of knowing who God is and who we are in relation to Him. We can take courage in the Lord, not because of who we are or what we have, but because of His indwelling presence with us through the Holy Spirit. By ourselves we are weak and can do nothing. But because He dwells in us, we have *His* power, wisdom, and courage. As we walk with Him, we understand more and more how much He loves us, and He begins to reveal His heart to us. We can take courage from these things. Courage arises from confidence in the vision the Lord has given to us; it comes from the quiet place of contemplation before the Lord where He visits us and speaks to us. Courage comes out of glorying in our own weakness and resting in His strength.

Courage also means taking one step at a time without demanding to know the complete journey up front. We tend to want to have everything mapped out in advance so we can know what we're getting into before we start. God rarely works that way. He says, "I'm not going to tell you what it looks like at the end. I'm giving you insight for right now. Trust Me and follow Me." There is a reason He does this: Walking one step at a time builds faith. God knows that our puny little brains can't handle the whole picture all at once. Sometimes God speaks things to us that seem so overwhelming that we can't see how in the world He will ever do it. Yet, He pours out His grace and leads us one step at a time. We take that step and then watch for the Lord to open a doorway of grace to enable us to take the next step and the next and the next. As we walk this way, our faith grows and so does our courage.

Our Testimony

In the Book of Revelation, John, the beloved apostle, presents a powerful picture of the victory that lies ahead for the bold and courageous Church:

Then war broke out in heaven; Michael and his angels went forth to battle with the dragon, and the dragon and his angels fought. But they were defeated, and there was no room found for them in heaven any longer. And the huge dragon was cast down and out— that age-old serpent, who is called the Devil and Satan, he who is the seducer (deceiver) of all humanity the world over; he was forced out and down to the earth, and his angels were flung out along with him. Then I heard a strong (loud) voice in heaven, saying, Now it has come—the salvation and the power and the kingdom (the dominion, the reign) of our God, and the power (the sovereignty, the authority) of His Christ (the Messiah); for the accuser of our brethren, he who keeps bringing before our God charges against them day and night, has been cast out! And they have overcome (conquered) him by means of the blood of the Lamb and by the utterance of their testimony, for they did not love and cling to life even when faced with death [holding their lives cheap till they had to die for their witnessing] (Revelation 12:7-11).

Satan and his angels were defeated and cast out of Heaven; never again could he accuse the brethren. It is the brethren—all

27

believers—who have overcome satan. How did this happen? They overcame "by means of the blood of the Lamb and by the utterance of their testimony."

Often when believers get together, the pastor or another leader will ask if anyone has a testimony to give. (Sometimes it is easy to get people to share; sometimes it isn't. A lot of it depends on how the Spirit is moving in the meeting and how He has moved recently in the lives of the people attending.) A testimony is simply a telling of what God has done or is doing in your life. Your testimony may seem small and insignificant in your mind compared to others that you hear, but it is still important. There may be someone who needs to hear just exactly the word from the Lord that your testimony would give them.

There is great power in our testimonies—power to defeat and overcome the enemy. The power lies in what Christ accomplished for us on the cross. Satan and his legions cannot stand against that kind of power. That is why it is important for us to share our testimonies, to tell of God's faithfulness and of His showing Himself strong on our behalf. It doesn't matter if the event is big or little; if God does it, we should tell it. The more we tell it, the more we take the chains off ourselves and off those who hear us, and put those chains where they belong: on the enemy.

When you step out with His banner of love and faithfulness over you, with the blessings of His grace, mercy, forgiveness, and healing upon you, and with the boldness and authority of His Word on your lips, you can face the world and the enemy with confidence and courage. No weapon that the enemy can fashion against you will stand because the power and purpose of God cannot be defeated. You have an unbeatable combination in the Word of God—"This is what the Lord says..."—along with the word of your testimony: "Let me tell you what the Lord has done for me...."

Satan will try to intimidate you with all sorts of things to keep your mouth shut. He'll try to convince you that it isn't important or that no one will be interested or that you were mistaken in thinking it was God who did it. Shoot down all those attacks with the weapons that God has given. Instead of being intimidated, claim the divine boldness that is yours by right as a child of God. You have to have the courage and faith to open your mouth and speak your testimony. God will do the rest. He hasn't called you to be successful—only faithful. When you are *faithful*, He will bring about success through you.

The chapters that follow profile nine ordinary Christian women who displayed extraordinary courage in following the call of God on their lives. Because they were faithful, God used them to accomplish extraordinary things. We can take courage from their examples. If God could use them, He can use us.

Chapter 3

The Cost of Courage

Some of you may think that you are the most unlikely candidate for God to use to do anything significant. Most of us think of ourselves in that way. The world teaches us that it is the rich, the powerful, or the beautiful who are important and make a difference in the world. That's not what God teaches. He doesn't think or work the way the world does. The prophet Isaiah recorded, "For My thoughts are not your thoughts, neither are your ways My ways, says the Lord. For as the heavens are higher than the earth, so are My ways higher than your ways and My thoughts than your thoughts" (Is. 55:8-9).

I like the way Randy Clark puts it: "God can use little ole me!" Yes, God can use anyone or anything He desires to accomplish His purpose. In fact, He prefers to use people and means considered insignificant by the world. The apostle Paul told the Corinthians:

...God selected (deliberately chose) what in the world is foolish to put the wise to shame, and what the world calls weak to put the strong to shame. And God also selected (deliberately chose) what in the world is low-born and insignificant and branded and treated with contempt, even the things that are nothing, that He might

depose and bring to nothing the things that are (1 Corinthians 1:27-28).

If in spite of these words you still wonder whether or not God can or will use you (as long as you make yourself available to Him), you can take courage, as I have, from the story of a young woman who was, humanly speaking, one of the most unlikely heroes in history: Joan of Arc. Her life has been a tremendous tool of inspiration to me in the past few years. May the shadow of courage of Joan's life fall upon you as well!

A Time for Leadership

The fourteenth and fifteenth centuries were years of great political and national turmoil for France. From 1337 to 1453 France and England fought a series of battles that became known as the Hundred Years War. At stake was the territory of Aquitane, a rich land in southwestern France that had been under English control since the twelfth century. France wanted it back; England was determined to keep it.[1] In addition, in 1338 King Edward III of England, through his mother a direct descendant of King Philip IV of France, claimed title to the French throne, thus setting off conflict between the two nations over royal succession in France.

By 1380, when King Charles V of France died, the situation had stabilized somewhat and a lasting peace seemed possible. The king's son, Charles VI, was only 12 years old when his father died. He was put under the guardianship of a ducal council until 1388, when he began ruling in his own right. He married Isabella of Bavaria and ruled well until 1392 when he had his first bout with the insanity that plagued the remainder of his reign. During these times Isabella served as his regent, and in effect she ruled in her husband's place. Charles' insanity and the resulting internal power struggle weakened the kingdom. The English eventually took advantage of the turmoil and invaded France.

The Cost of Courage

In 1415 King Henry V of England inflicted a devastating defeat on the French at Agincourt, leaving the country divided into three parts. In 1420, Isabella, serving as regent for her mad husband, signed the Treaty of Troyes. This treaty, among other things, secured for Henry V accession to the French throne upon the death of Charles VI. At the same time, courting Henry's favor, Isabella disowned her own son, the dauphin, Charles VII, and gave her daughter Catherine to Henry in marriage. All this strengthened Henry's claim to the French throne. Thus Charles VII, the otherwise legitimate heir to the throne of France, was cut off.

Around 1400 an ancient French prophecy was revived that said the kingdom would be brought to ruin by a woman and restored by a daughter of the people. Many came to believe that Isabella had fulfilled the first part of the prophecy when she signed the Treaty of Troyes, giving the French throne to the English king.[2] But who would be the "daughter of the people" who would arise to restore the kingdom?

The situation in France was made worse in 1422 when both Charles VI and Henry V died and Henry's infant son (Henry VI) was proclaimed king of both England and France. It was so bad in France that children died of hunger in the streets by the thousands. It is said that wolves even came into Paris at night to feed on the bodies of the unburied dead. There was great lawlessness and immorality and many people lived little better than beasts.[3] The disinherited Charles, from his base in central and southwestern France, attempted to assert his authority and claim to the throne, but with little success. The French people as a whole would not recognize him as the legitimate king unless he was formally coronated in the traditional place, the cathedral in the now English-controlled city of Rheims.[4]

If ever there was a time for a strong leader to arise, it was now. The time for courage had come!

An Unlikely Champion

It was in the midst of this political unrest and social upheaval that Joan appeared. Born in 1412 in the village of Domremy, in the Champagne district of northeastern France, Joan was the youngest in a family of five. Although skilled in sewing and spinning, she never learned to read or write. From a very early age she displayed an unusually deep devotion to God. She spent hours absorbed in prayer and was known to have a tender heart for the poor and needy.[5]

From her childhood on Joan simply loved God. She never received any theological training and knew very little about the formal structures and official doctrines of the Roman Catholic Church—the only church in France at that time. All Joan knew was that when she went to mass, God met her there. God can come into any church, any building, any worship setting—formal or informal—to meet with people who love Him and are hungry for His presence. Joan pressed forward in the avenue that God made available for her to experience Him. She knew God, loved to spend time with Him, and would do anything for Him.

In the summer of 1425, when she was 13, Joan experienced her first heavenly visitation: a blaze of bright light accompanied by a voice. She received numerous such visitations during the months that followed and gradually discerned the identities of those who spoke to her. Joan identified one of them as Michael the archangel; St. Catherine of Alexandria and St. Margaret of Antioch, both early Christian martyrs, were the others.[6] Although these may seem to be strange messengers to modern minds, remember that, in the case of Michael, angelic visitations have biblical precedent. As for the other two, it is natural that Joan would have understood and interpreted her visitors in a manner consistent with the religious environment of her day. From the historical records of her life, her trial and execution, and her later rehabilitation, in my understanding there is little doubt today of the divine nature of her visitations.

The Cost of Courage

At first Joan's "voices" told her such things as, "Be a good girl and obey your parents." However, over the course of three years the messages began to change. She had dreams of horses running in battle and of herself being led away with an army of men. During this time she gradually became aware of the call of God on her life. He seemed to be telling her that she was to go to the aid of the disinherited Charles, the true king of France; drive the English away from Orleans and out of the country; and lead the procession to see Charles enthroned. At first she resisted: "I'm just a girl. I have no education, no training in military skills. Who's going to listen to me?" Her voices continued, however, and became more and more insistent.

By May 1428 Joan was convinced beyond a shadow of a doubt that God was leading her to go to Charles' aid. Her life of fellowship and communion with the Lord had been such that once she was convinced of her call, the vision so convicted and consumed her that she let nothing stand in her way. She had such a concrete understanding of who her Father was and loved Him so much that she would go anywhere and do anything to fulfill His desire. Nothing was too great a task for Him to ask of her. She believed that God was true and that He would back her up in everything that He called her to do.

A Divine Mission

A month later, under the insistent direction of her "voices," Joan presented herself and her mission to Robert Baudricourt, the commander of Charles' forces in the neighboring town of Vaucouleurs. Baudricourt showed little other than contempt for Joan and her ideas, telling the cousin who had accompanied her to "Take her home to her father and give her a good whipping."[7] Joan returned to Domremy, apparently defeated.

In the meantime, Charles' situation worsened as the English beseiged the city of Orleans on October 12, 1428. By the end of the year, total defeat for the French seemed near at hand. Joan's visitations continued, her "voices" becoming increasingly urgent. When she tried to resist, they told her, "It is God who commands it." Finally, in January 1429, Joan returned to Vaucouleurs for another try.[8]

This time, she stayed in the town and gradually made an impression on Baudricourt. According to one account, he waved a sword in her face, saying, "What do your 'voices' say to this?" In response, Joan grabbed a short, dagger-like sword from a nearby attendant and brought its blade down against the blade of Baudricourt's sword, severing it as if it were paper. Baudricourt then arranged for her to see Charles and sent Joan with a three-man escort to Chinon, where Charles was staying. Joan traveled in men's clothing, probably for modesty and practicality.

Charles, not knowing what to make of this teenage girl who was coming to see him, decided to test Joan by disguising himself and surrounding himself with attendants. However, when Joan was brought in, she somehow immediately recognized him and addressed him as the king. Despite this, Charles was still skeptical. Joan offered to prove that she had been sent by God by answering for Charles three questions that were known only to him and to God: whether or not he was the true heir to the French throne, that if France's troubles were because of his sins that he alone be punished and the nation spared, and that if the war was due to the sins of the people that they be forgiven and the troubles lifted.[9] Joan's divinely inspired insight convinced Charles, at least half-heartedly, to believe in her mission.

Before she was entrusted with military operations, however, Joan was sent to the city of Poitiers where she was examined by a large committee of highly educated bishops and doctors. This illiterate young woman held her own against the searching and deep questions put to her. In the end, her faith, simplicity, and honesty made a very positive impression on these learned theologians, who found nothing heretical in her claims of supernatural guidance.[10]

The Cost of Courage

Returning to Chinon, Joan began preparing for her campaign. It was at this early stage that two significant events occurred that appeared to confirm even more the divine nature of her mission. Joan needed a sword, and she knew where to find one. She wrote to the priests at the chapel of Saint Catherine of Fierbois, informing them that her sword was buried behind the altar. Indeed, the sword was found at that exact spot.[11]

The second event involved a letter, which still exists, written on April 22, 1429, and delivered and duly registered before any of the events referred to in the letter took place. The writer of the letter reported that Joan had said that she would deliver the city of Orleans; she would compel the English to raise the seige; she herself would be wounded, but would survive; and Charles would be crowned king before the end of the summer.[12] As it turned out, all of these things were fulfilled just as Joan predicted.

An Army of the Lord

Joan had such an incredible presence of the Lord on her that she drew people to her everywhere she turned. By the time she arrived on the field, Charles' army was at a very low point; they were exhausted, defeated, discouraged, and disillusioned. Many of the soldiers had begun to desert. Then Joan appeared, proclaiming, "I have a vision from God. He has called me to raise an army for our nation and for Him." As Joan's presence became known, soldiers began to rush to her side by the thousands. The call was given and they came gladly. Rough, vulgar, immoral, and intemperate though many of them were, the men found her innocence, spiritual piety, and patriotic fervor irresistible. Her presence filled them with new vigor and courage. She held up for them a standard of righteousness, purity, and devotion to the Lord, and they rallied around her. Even though she was a young woman in the midst of an army of men, Joan had a holy quality about her that repressed all tendencies to regard her in a sexual manner.

Joan made clear what the requirements were for being a part of her "army of the Lord." First, she told the soldiers that the camp prostitutes had to go. Second, the soldiers had to attend mass every day. Third, there was to be no more cursing or swearing. Amazingly, Joan's influence was so great that her army embraced these standards enthusiastically. As miraculous as it seems, they agreed as one body to come into holy living and purity.

Joan had absolutely no training in military operations or strategy, but God gave her battle plans on the field. Some of the generals were still not completely convinced, however, and tried to trick her by following other strategies. God revealed to Joan what was going on and she challenged the generals: "In God's Name, the advice of Our Lord is wiser and more certain than yours. You thought to deceive me, but it is you who are deceived, for I bring you the best help that ever came to any soldier or to any city."[13] The conviction from her words pierced their hearts like an arrow.

After the English rejected a demand from Joan that they leave French soil, Joan and her army moved rapidly and entered the city of Orleans on April 30, 1429. Within a week they had captured all the English forts surrounding the city. Although Joan was wounded in the breast by an arrow on the last day of battle, she was insistent on pressing forward with the campaign. One reason for this was her warlike instinct. The other was that her "voices" had already told her that she had only one year. She knew time was important.[14]

Joan's insistence prevailed against the reluctance of the king and his advisers. A short campaign along the Loire River led to a great victory on June 18 at Patay where English reinforcements sent from Paris were completely defeated. Joan pressed on, still laboring to overcome the reluctance of the commanders. Nevertheless, they captured the city of Troyes, opening the way to Rheims where, on July 17, 1429, Charles VII was solemnly crowned king with Joan standing by as a witness.[15]

The Cost of Courage

Reversal and Betrayal

Although the principal purpose of her mission had been accomplished, Joan remained with the army throughout the rest of the summer. An attempt to retake Paris from the English failed and in a later battle Joan was wounded again, this time in the thigh. The king signed a truce with the Duke of Burgundy, who was allied with the English, and there was no further fighting until the following year.

Joan spent a miserable winter among the worldliness and jealousy of the king's court. On December 29, 1429, Charles ennobled Joan and her entire family, perhaps partly in an attempt to console her. She was probably more than ready when she took to the battlefield the following April when the truce ended.[16]

Her "voices" continued to speak to her, telling her that she would be taken prisoner before Midsummer Day. This happened on the evening of May 24, 1430, while Joan and troops under her command were defending the city of Compeigne against Burgundian attack. The commander of the city accidentally raised the drawbridge while Joan and many of her soldiers were still outside. She was pulled from her horse and made a prisoner of war.[17]

Although they had several important English prisoners whom they could have traded for Joan, Charles VII and his advisors did nothing to try to rescue her. The English, on the other hand, were desperate to get their hands on her. They both feared and hated her because of the defeat and embarrassment they had suffered at her hands and were determined somehow to take her life. The English struck a deal with Joan's Burgundian captors, who sold her for a sum of money that today would equal hundreds of thousands of dollars.[18]

Trial and Martyrdom

The English knew that they could not legitimately execute Joan simply because she had defeated them in battle. Instead, their strategy was to have her condemned to death as a witch and a heretic. To this end they claimed that Joan's "voices" were satanic in nature and that the only way she could have defeated them in battle was with the help of the powers of darkness. Joan's practice of wearing male dress was also used against her as evidence of her heresy.

The trial of Joan of Arc is one of the most thoroughly documented events of that period of history. After months of imprisonment in disgraceful conditions she was questioned intensively by the most learned theologians of the day. There is a complete record both of the questions she was asked and of her answers. Throughout the entire proceeding Joan's faith, integrity, and spiritual insight shone brightly. Isn't that what Jesus told His disciples to do—let their light shine and overcome darkness?

Imagine how you would feel in Joan's place: a young woman not yet out of your teens, unable to read or write and without any formal religious training of any kind, being examined and questioned about fine points of religion, faith, theology, and the Church by men determined to find something with which to condemn you. Yet Joan stood firm because God held her up. He was her defense and her strong tower and He gave her the wisdom and the words to answer every question. The record of her trial leaves little room to doubt either her absolute devotion to God or the courage with which she stood for Him. At a time when the institutional Church held almost absolute authority over the life and death of people, here is how Joan responded to questions regarding her spiritual allegiance:

Q: If the Church Militant tells you that your revelations are illusions, or diabolical things, will you defer to the Church?

A: I will defer to God, Whose Commandment I always do...In case the Church should prescribe the contrary, I should not refer to anyone in the world, but to God alone, Whose Commandment I always follow.

The Cost of Courage

Q: Do you not then believe you are subject to the Church of God which is on earth, that is to say to our Lord the Pope, to the Cardinals, the Archbishops, Bishops, and other prelates of the Church?

A: Yes, I believe myself to be subject to them, but God must be served first.

Q: Have you then command from your voices not to submit yourself to the Church Militant, which is on earth, not to its decision?

A: I answer nothing from my own head, what I answer is by command of my voices, they do not order me to disobey the Church, but God must be served first.[19]

In the end Joan was condemned to death for heresy. She signed a retraction that she probably did not fully understand and her sentence was changed to imprisonment for life. A few days later, however, she resumed wearing male dress in the prison, which gave her enemies the excuse to condemn her again as a "relapsed heretic." Joan was turned over for execution by burning at the stake. Sadly, that execution was carried out on May 30, 1431.

Joan's behavior when facing death was admirable, moving even her bitter enemies to tears. The normal practice when someone was burned at the stake was for the wood to be laid at the front and, after the flames and smoke had risen up, for the executioner to strangle the victim from behind. It was a merciful gesture intended to spare the victim the pain and agony of the burning. This practice was not followed in Joan's case. She faced the flames fully conscious. As the flames rose Joan called out for the cross. When it was held up before her, she called repeatedly on the name of Jesus, forgiving those who had wronged her and pouring out words of love and devotion to Him.

Apparently everyone who watched was deeply moved by her witness. Many were deeply convicted by what they had done, recognizing that Joan certainly could not have been a heretic. In fact, some were so convicted that they were moved to repentance and came to know the Lord on the spot. According to some accounts, some of the people claimed to have seen the name of Jesus written in the flames, while others said they saw a white dove fly out of the flames.[20] The executioner himself is reported to have said that Joan's heart would not burn.[21]

Twenty-five years after her death, Joan's case was reopened and the facts reexamined. As a result, Joan was declared to be completely innocent of all crimes, being neither a witch nor a heretic but a victim of jealousy, hatred, and political intrigue. For centuries she has been considered a French national heroine, and in 1920 the Catholic Church canonized her.[22]

Joan's Legacy

What does the life of this fifteenth century teenaged girl have to say to us today?

First, I believe that we can take courage from the simple fact that Joan was so ordinary. There was nothing obvious that made her stand out. By normal human standards she had no qualifications for the mission she undertook. She had no education, no religious training, no leadership experience. She was not ordained to the ministry. In fact, she lived during a time when women's freedom in both Church and society was greatly restricted.

What made the difference? Joan possessed the only qualification that mattered: She loved God with all her heart, soul, mind, and strength. She was completely sold out to Him. God chose her and used her because she made herself available to Him. Her executioner claimed that her heart would not burn. If this was so, perhaps it was because her heart had already been burned by her passion for God. She was so consumed by Him that nothing else could touch her. We can all take courage from the fact that the only thing God requires from us in order for Him to use us is that we know Him, love Him, and make ourselves available to Him. God's army is an army of *volunteers*.

The Cost of Courage

The standards Joan laid down for her army show us that the Lord has called His army (us) to a life of purity, holiness, and complete devotion to Him. If we are to be effective and fully usable, we must put away all filth and uncleanness, all sin and evil thinking, and be clean vessels before the Lord. God has raised His standard of righteousness for us to rally under and has told us, "You shall be holy, for I am holy" (1 Pet. 1:16b). The apostle Paul expressed it well when he wrote,

> I appeal to you therefore, brethren, and beg of you in view of [all] the mercies of God, to make a decisive dedication of your bodies [presenting all your members and faculties] as a living sacrifice, holy (devoted, consecrated) and well pleasing to God, which is your reasonable (rational, intelligent) service and spiritual worship (Romans 12:1).

We must be blameless in our behavior, wholesome in our speech, and consistent in our walk.

Regardless of what the world tries to do to us, we can walk blameless and undefiled before God. The purity and holiness that He places in us can come out as an extension of us, and we can then pass them on to other people. We don't have to be tainted by the world. On the contrary, we can influence the world for Christ. It isn't easy, and it costs everything, but with God's help it can be done. And He receives the glory!

Joan's example encourages us to dare to believe that we can do whatever God calls us to do. It assures us that He will back us up in our call and bring it to pass as we obey and follow Him. It is inconceivable that Joan could have done what she did without the hand of God on her life. One thing that the Lord told Joan again and again was, "Go on! Go on, daughter of God! Go on; I will be with you and I will be your help." He says the same thing to us today: "Go on into your destiny, into your calling, into your place before the Lord. Go on! Push through! Endure! Let Me show Myself strong on your behalf."

43

God is looking for men and women who will be sold out to Him; He wants people who will let their hearts and minds be so consumed with Him that nothing else matters. All that mattered to Joan was reaching Rheims and seeing her king crowned according to God's will. Doing so required pressing through the heart of the English army, moving through the hardest and greatest difficulties to reach the place of victory. It is the same for us. We need to go to the place that is the most difficult for us, where the enemy seems to have the greatest stronghold, and enthrone Jesus there. We need to raise His banner and make a way for Him to come and receive the honor due His name.

The cost to Joan for courage was her life, but her reward was the company and presence of God and the fulfillment of His purpose in and through her. To have courage will cost us everything as well: our whole lives given completely to the Lord in sacrifice and devotion. What is our reward? Life! We want to proclaim life, not death; blessing, not cursing; and light, not darkness. However, it is only in losing our life that we find it. And what we find is His life, not ours.

Courage is not something we can drum up from within ourselves; it comes from knowing God and trusting Him completely. As we learn to depend on Him rather than on ourselves, He releases His power in and through us—and that power can change our families, our friends, our communities, our nation, and even the whole world. God is not a respecter of persons. If He used someone as ordinary as Joan of Arc, He will use you too! Dare to believe!

When visiting Paris, France, with my husband Jim, we toured Notre Dame Cathedral. There we stumbled upon a statue of Joan of Arc, and I had my picture taken standing at Joan's side. I want to be a woman of courage and walk in the footsteps where others have trodden. Does this echo the cry of your heart? Then continue on with me as we turn the pages to look at the lives of other women of courage, beginning with Perpetua, a courageous martyr for her faith.

The Cost of Courage

Endnotes

1. U.X.L.® Biographies. "Joan of Arc." 1996. 22 SEP 98 <http://www.gale.com/gale/cwh/joan.html>.
2. C.M. Stevens, *The Wonderful Story of Joan of Arc and the Meaning of Her Life for Americans* (New York: Cupples and Leon Company, 1918), 28.
3. Stevens, *The Wonderful Song*, 29.
4. U.X.L.® Biographies. "Joan of Arc."
5. Herbert Thurston, "St. Joan of Arc," *The Catholic Encyclopedia* (Encyclopedia Press, Inc., 1913). Electronic version © 1996. 22 SEP 98 <http://www.knight.org/advent/cathen/08409c.htm>.
6. Thurston, "St. Joan of Arc."
7. Thurston, "St. Joan of Arc."
8. Thurston, "St. Joan of Arc."
9. Francis W. Leary, *The Golden Longing* (New York: Scribner, 1959), 31.
10. Thurston, "St. Joan of Arc."
11. Leary, *The Golden Longing*, 42.
12. Thurston, "St. Joan of Arc."
13. Leary, *The Golden Longing*, 44.
14. Thurston, "St. Joan of Arc."
15. Thurston, "St. Joan of Arc."
16. Thurston, "St. Joan of Arc."
17. Thurston, "St. Joan of Arc."
18. Thurston, "St. Joan of Arc."
19. I.I. Spirea, c. Counsel Quest™. "Joan of Arc Trial Transcripts." 1994-1998. 29 OCT 98 <http://www.counselquest.com/Joan-of-Arc.htm>.
20. Stevens, *The Wonderful Story*, 300.
21. Stevens, *The Wonderful Story*, 302.
22. U.X.L.® Biographies. "Joan of Arc."

Part II

Women of Courage

Chapter 4

Vibia Perpetua: Faithful Unto Death

I saw a golden ladder which reached from earth to the heavens; but so narrow, that only one could mount it at a time. To the two sides were fastened all sorts of iron instruments, as swords, lances, hooks, and knives; so that if any one went up carelessly he was in great danger of having his flesh torn by those weapons. At the foot of the ladder lay a dragon of an enormous size, who kept guard to turn back and terrify those that endeavored to mount it. The first that went up was Saturus, who was not apprehended with us, but voluntarily surrendered himself afterwards on our account: when he was got to the top of the ladder, he turned towards me and said: "Perpetua, I wait for you; but take care lest the dragon bite you." I answered: "In the name of our Lord Jesus Christ, he shall not hurt me." Then the dragon, as if afraid of me, gently lifted his head from under the ladder, and I, having got upon the first step, set my foot upon his head. Thus I mounted to the top, and there I saw a garden of an immense space, and in the middle of it a tall man sitting down dressed like a shepherd, having white hair. He was milking his sheep, surrounded with many thousands of persons clad in white. He called me by my name, bid me welcome, and gave me some curds made of the milk which he had drawn: I put my hands together and took and ate them; and all that were present said aloud, Amen. The noise awaked me, chewing something very sweet. As soon as I had related to my brother this vision, we both concluded that we should suffer death.[1]

With these words Vibia Perpetua, a young noblewoman of Carthage in northern Africa, recorded a vision that she received from God in response to her prayer asking whether or not she faced martyrdom. Her question was quite relevant, for at the time of her vision Perpetua and five others were in prison; they were charged with defying Emperor Septimus Severus' prohibition against conversions to Christianity. The year was A.D. 203, and a general persecution that had begun a few years earlier in the European part of the Roman Empire had finally reached Africa.

Perpetua's companions in prison were a slave named Revocatus; his fellow-slave, Felicitas, who was seven months pregnant; and two freemen, Saturninus and Secundulus. All five were catechumens; that is, they were new believers who were being instructed in doctrine and discipline before being admitted to baptism and church membership. As it happened, they all received baptism while in prison. They were joined in prison by their instructor in the faith, Saturus (the one mentioned in Perpetua's vision), who, although not present when the others were arrested, had given himself up voluntarily in order to be with them during their ordeal.

An Allegiance Higher Than Family

Vibia Perpetua, 22 years old, came from a good family and had married a man of quality in Carthage, although he is strangely absent in the existing accounts of her imprisonment and martyrdom. It is possible that Perpetua was a widow, since she released her infant son into the care of her mother, though the child was brought to her regularly for nursing, and since apparently her

Vibia Perpetua: Faithful Unto Death

death would make the child an orphan. Perpetua's two surviving brothers (a third had died as a child) were believers, as was her mother, but her father was a pagan. He loved Perpetua more than all his other children and made several attempts to persuade her to recant or deny her Christian faith in order to spare her life.

One day shortly after her imprisonment began Perpetua's father visited her, appealing to her for the sake of her life and for that of her nursing baby to renounce her faith. Pointing to a water-pot or some other container, Perpetua asked her father, "Can that vessel, which you see, change its name?" When he answered that it could not, Perpetua said to him, "Nor can I call myself any other than I am, that is to say, a Christian."[2]

On another occasion, as Perpetua's trial before the Roman procurator approached, her father tried again. In Perpetua's own words:

> My father came over from the city worn out with exhaustion, and he went up to me in order to deflect me, saying: "My daughter, have pity on my white hairs! Show some compassion to your father, if I deserve to be called father by you....do not bring me into disgrace in all men's eyes! Look at your brothers, look at your mother and your aunt—look at your son, who won't be able to live if you die. Don't flaunt your insistence, or you'll destroy us all: for if anything happens to you, none of us will ever be able to speak freely and openly again."

> This is what my father said, out of devotion to me, kissing my hands and flinging himself at my feet; and amid his tears he called me not "daughter" but "domina" [my lady]. And I grieved for my father's condition—for he alone of all my family would not gain joy from my ordeal. And I comforted him, saying: "At the tribunal things will go as God wills: for you must know that we are no longer in our own hands, but in God's." And he left me griefstricken.[3]

A short time later, as Perpetua stood before Hilarian, the procurator of the province, her father made a final attempt.

Apparently Perpetua was the last of the prisoners to be examined because she records that all those who were questioned ahead of her boldly confessed Jesus Christ. When it was her turn, her father suddenly appeared, carrying her infant son. He appealed to her motherly instinct, begging her to consider the misery that she would bring on her son if she persisted. Even the judge Hilarian joined in, saying, "What! Will neither the gray hairs of a father you are going to make miserable, nor the tender innocence of a child, which your death will leave an orphan, move you? Sacrifice for the prosperity of the emperor."

Perpetua replied, "I will not do it."

Hilarian asked her directly, "Are you then a Christian?"

"Yes, I am."

After this reply the judge sentenced Perpetua and all her companions to be exposed to wild beasts at the emperor's festival games.[4]

A Vision of Victory

Secundulus apparently died in prison, but Perpetua and the others faced their impending deaths with anticipation. In the spirit of the apostles of the New Testament, they rejoiced that they were considered worthy to suffer for their Lord (see Acts 5:41). During the final days before the games, the Lord encouraged each of them through dreams and visions that assured them of victory and of His presence with them throughout. In Perpetua's vision, a deacon named Pomponius led her to the center of the amphitheater, encouraging her to not be afraid. Then, according to Perpetua:

I saw much people watching closely. And because I knew that I was condemned to the beasts I marveled that beasts were not sent out against me. And there came out against me a certain ill-favored Egyptian with his helpers to fight me. Also there came to me comely young men, my helpers and aiders. And I was stripped naked and I became a man. And my helpers began to rub me with oil as their custom is for a contest; and over against me saw that Egyptian wallowing in the dust. And there came forth a man of very great stature, so that he overpassed the very top of the amphitheater...bearing a rod like a master of gladiators, and a green branch whereon were golden apples. And he besought silence and said: The Egyptian, if shall conquer this woman, shall slay her with the sword; and if she shall conquer him, she shall receive this branch....[The Egyptian] tried to trip up my feet, but I with my heels smote upon his face. And I rose up into the air and began so to smite him as though I trod not the earth....And I caught his head, and he fell upon his face; and I trod upon his head. And the people began to shout, and my helpers began to sing. And I went up to the master of gladiators and received the branch. And he kissed me and said to me: Daughter, peace be with you. And I began to go with glory to the gate called the Gate of Life.

And I awoke; and I understood that I should fight, not with beasts but against the devil; but I knew that mine was the victory.[5]

Isn't that what we are called to do as well? Fight! Yes, we are to fight the good fight of faith.

Courage and Faithfulness

By all accounts Perpetua and her companions remained steadfast in faith and witness throughout the days of their imprisonment and on the day they met their deaths in the arena. In fact, the keeper of the prison, a man named Pudens, was himself converted to Christ by the faithful testimony of his prisoners.

During the customary final meal, which was eaten in public, the Christians did their best to turn the affair into an *Agape-* or Love-feast, talking freely with the crowd that was watching them, testifying to Christ, threatening the judgments of God, and rejoicing in their own sufferings. Their steadfast faith and courage so impressed the onlookers that several of them were converted.

On the day of the games, the condemned marched from the prison to the amphitheater, joy in their eyes and characterizing their every word and gesture. The two women, Perpetua and Felicitas, walked together. An eyewitness wrote that "Perpetua walked with a composed countenance and easy pace, as a woman cherished by Jesus Christ, with her eyes modestly cast down."[6] Felicitas was especially joyful to be with her friends because it had appeared for a while that her pregnancy would prevent her from dying with them, for Roman law forbade the execution of pregnant women. This had upset her greatly, but through her prayers and the prayers of her friends, she had while in prison safely delivered a daughter. The baby was then taken into the home of a Christian woman who would raise the child as her own.

As they reached the gate of the arena, they were given the customary robes to wear that had been consecrated to the Roman gods. The condemned Christians refused to wear the idolatrous clothing, however. Perpetua forcefully stood her ground, telling the Roman tribune that they had agreed to come of their own accord on the promise that they would not be forced to do anything contrary to their religion. The tribune allowed them to proceed in their own clothes.

Revocatus and Saturninus were dispatched rather quickly after being attacked first by a leopard and then by a bear. Saturus' death took a little longer. He was exposed first to a wild boar, which promptly turned on and fatally wounded its keeper. Then it did nothing more than drag Saturus. Next he was exposed to a bear, which refused to come out of its den. Finally, Saturus died from a single bite of a leopard.

Perpetua and Felicitas were exposed to a wild cow that, when it attacked, tossed first Perpetua and then Felicitas. Perpetua landed on her back, then sat up and gathered her torn clothes about her to preserve her modesty. She stood up, tied up her hair, which had fallen loose, and helped the badly mauled Felicitas to her feet. They stood together, expecting another assault from the cow when the crowd cried out that it was enough. Perpetua and Felicitas were then taken to the Gate of Life, which is where victims who survived the beasts were put to death by gladiators. The two women exchanged a final kiss of peace.

The gladiator assigned to execute Perpetua was a novice, young and very nervous. He was shaking so much that he was able to inflict only a few painful but not deadly wounds. Perpetua herself then calmly guided his hand and sword to her own neck where he then finished the job.

Perpetua's Legacy

There are several remarkable things about Perpetua and her martyrdom that can encourage us. First, the existing account of her imprisonment, trial, and death is regarded as reliably historical (as compared to some other martyr accounts that contain much legend) and is one of the earliest historical accounts of Christianity after the close of the New Testament. The fact that much of the story was written by Perpetua herself makes it one of the earliest pieces of writing by a Christian woman. The story was so highly regarded that it was read widely in African churches for the next several centuries and was treated as almost equivalent to Scripture.

Perpetua faced her martyrdom with a confidence and courage that did not come strictly from within herself, but was given to her by the Lord whom she so faithfully gave witness to. Her experience is full of evidence of how Christ sustained her and the others throughout their ordeal. He never abandoned them, but remained close to them. They drew constant strength from His presence. Jesus is the same yesterday, today, and forever (see Heb. 13:8), and what He did for them He will do for us. He has promised never to leave us or forsake us (see Heb. 13:5).

Her courage inspires us even more when we remember that she and all the others, with the possible exception of Saturus, were *new* believers; it was only after they were in prison that they received baptism. They were in the early stages of learning the doctrines and disciplines of the faith. This shows us that what counts ultimately is our commitment to Christ, not knowledge. Knowledge of our faith is very important, but knowledge alone does not give us the courage to stand firm. That comes only through the Person and presence of Jesus Christ in our lives.

Essentially, Perpetua was no different from any of us. She was an ordinary woman who trusted Christ completely and was given the courage and confidence to be faithful unto death. As we learn to trust Christ, we will find that He gives us the courage and confidence as well to meet whatever challenges come our way.

Maybe you aren't called to be a martyr for your faith, but each of us is called to die to self. It takes courage to die! May we learn how to gain strength for the journey from the example of this legend from Church history—Perpetua, faithful unto death.

Now let's walk in another woman's shoes and view the life and testimony of Sojourner Truth, one of America's woman evangelists.

Endnotes

1. Alban Butler, "St. Perpetua, and Felicitas, mm. with their Companions," *The Lives of the Fathers, Martyrs and Other Principal Saints* (D. & J. Sadlier & Company, 1864). 1 SEP 1998 <http://www.cin.org/saints/pet&fel.html>.
2. Terry Matz, "Perpetua and Felicity," *Catholic Online Saints*. 7 March 1996 <http://www.catholic.org/saints/perp.htm>.
3. Peter Dronke, trans. "Perpetua," *Women Writers of the Middle Ages* (Cambridge Univ. Press, 1984). <http://www.millersv. edu/~english/homepage/duncan/medfem/pertext.html>.
4. Butler, "St. Perpetua."

5. W.H. Shewring, trans., *The Passion of Perpetua and Felicity* (London, 1931). *Internet Medieval Sourcebook*. 1 SEP 1998 <http://www.fordham.edu/halsall/source/perpetua.html>.
6. Butler, "St. Perpetua."

Chapter 5

Sojourner Truth: "Ain't I a Woman?"

On November 28, 1883, a crowd of nearly a thousand people gathered before a modest house in Battle Creek, Michigan, to pay their final respects to one of the most remarkable American women of the nineteenth century. Silently, on foot and in carriages, they fell into line behind the hearse bearing the body of Sojourner Truth: ex-slave, mother, evangelist, abolitionist, author, women's rights advocate, temperance activist, and proponent of land grant benefits for ex-slaves. Her coffin borne by white residents of Battle Creek, the 86-year-old African-American was laid to rest in the Oakhill Cemetery. Many of her friends from the women's rights and abolitionist movements spoke of her "rare qualities of head and heart" and remembered her as a "dynamic woman with strength, integrity, poise, and wit."[1]

As an adult she was a powerful public speaker, captivating her mostly white audiences wherever she went. No one who met her or heard her speak ever forgot her. Nearly six feet tall with a deep, powerful voice, Sojourner Truth was an imposing presence. Never one to back down from a challenge, she was one of the first black women in the United States to win a court case, which she did not once, but three times. Her influence brought her into contact with many important leaders of the day, both religious and political. She even had private meetings with three U.S. presidents.

What makes the accomplishments of this formidable woman even more amazing is that throughout her long life she was illiterate. Even though she published an autobiography and knew large portions of the Bible by heart, Sojourner Truth, like Joan of Arc centuries before her, never learned how to read or write.

From Slavery to Freedom

Named Isabella by her parents but called "Bell," Sojourner Truth was born to a slave couple on a farm in upstate New York around 1797. From the beginning her parents instilled in her the importance and value of hard work. Bell's mother also taught her to pray to God during times of trouble. Bell learned both lessons well even though she didn't think about God very much while she was growing up and, as a slave, had little opportunity to learn about Him.

By the time she was in her mid-20's, Bell had belonged to five different masters. She had married another slave named Tom and had given birth to five children. In 1824 Bell heard the news that the New York state legislature had passed a law abolishing slavery in the state. Under the terms of the law she and Tom would become free on July 4, 1827. In 1825 John Dumont, Bell's owner of 15 years, was impressed with her hard work and offered her a deal: If she worked extra hard for the next year, he would free her and Tom a year early. Bell accepted eagerly and did her part. At the end of the year, however, a poor harvest caused Dumont to feel he could not afford to free them as he had promised. Feeling betrayed, Bell determined to run away, even though by law she would be free in another year.

Sojourner Truth: "Ain't I a Woman?"

Bell wondered when to make her attempt. Running away during the day would be foolish, and she was afraid of the dark. As her mother had taught her, Bell prayed to God, and He showed her what to do: leave around dawn, while everyone else was still asleep but there was enough light to see. Taking her youngest child, Sophia, Bell fled to the home of a Quaker couple a few miles away who gave them shelter. When Dumont found them there the next day, Bell refused to return. The Quaker couple bought her and Sophia from Dumont for $25, then promptly set them free.

Bell looked forward to the day when all her family would be free. But before that day arrived, Dumont sold her only son, Peter, to a doctor who found the boy unsuitable to his needs. The doctor turned Peter over to his brother, who sold Peter to an Alabama planter. Bell was furious because Alabama was a "slave-for-life" state. She was determined, whatever the cost, to get her son back.

Encouraged by her Quaker friends, Bell sought legal action to have Peter returned. An attorney assured her that Peter's out-of-state sale was illegal and began to work on her behalf. Things looked promising, but then were delayed because court was not in session. Bell was too impatient to wait. Her lawyer asked her to be patient with the court system.

While walking home that day, Bell cried out to Jesus to intercede for her before the throne of God. Her prayer was answered when she met a perfect stranger on the road who asked her if her son had been returned yet. When she said no, the stranger pointed to a nearby house and told her that an attorney lived there who could help her. Bell went to see him, and within 24 hours the court had returned Peter to her. For the rest of her life Bell testified that she was certain that the stranger she had met on the road was sent from God to help her.[2]

61

"This Is Jesus!"

Under the provisions of New York's emancipation law, slaves born after July 4, 1799, were freed when they reached a particular age: 28 for men and 25 for women. For this reason Bell's other three daughters remained on the Dumont farm, where she could visit them regularly. After a while Bell settled her differences with the Dumonts and sent Sophia there to live with her sisters while Bell and Peter lived with the Quaker couple who had originally helped her.

For years before her freedom Bell had prayed to God for help in becoming free, promising that if He helped her, she would try to be good and remember to pray. Once she was free, however, and things began to settle down, she forgot about God. Then, on a festival day, John Dumont brought a wagon and invited Bell to visit her family on his farm. What happened next was a pivotal event in Bell's life. Years later, Sojourner Truth described the event to Harriet Beecher Stowe, the author of *Uncle Tom's Cabin*, who wrote it down:

> Well, jest as I was goin' out to git into the wagon, I MET GOD! An' says I, "O God, I didn't know as you was so great!" An' I turned right round an' come into the house, an' set down in my room; for 'twas God all around me. I could feel it burnin', burnin', burnin' all around me, an' goin' through me; an' I saw I was so wicked, it seemed as ef it would burn me up. An' I said, "O somebody, somebody, stand between God an' me! for it burns me!" Then, honey, when I said so, I felt as it were somethin' like an amberill [umbrella] that came between me an' the light, an' I felt it was SOMEBODY,—somebody that stood between me an' God; an' it felt cool, like a shade; an' says I, "Who's this that stands between me an' God?"...I begun to feel 'twas somebody that loved me; an' I tried to know him....An' finally somethin' spoke out in me an' said, "THIS IS JESUS!" An' I spoke out with all my might, an' says I, "THIS IS JESUS! Glory be to God!" An' then the whole world grew bright, an' the trees they waved an' waved

in glory, an' every little bit o' stone on the ground shone like glass; an' I shouted an' said, "Praise, praise, praise to the Lord!" An' I begun to feel such a love in my soul as I never felt before,—love to all creatures. An' then, all of a sudden, it stopped, an' I said, "Dar's de white folks, that have abused you an' beat you an' abused your people,—think o' them!" But then there came another rush of love through my soul, an' I cried out loud,—"Lord, Lord, I can love EVEN DE WHITE FOLKS!"...I jes' walked round an' round in a dream. Jesus loved me! I knowed it,—I felt it. Jesus was my Jesus.[3]

Bell's conversion to Christ made a profound impact on her. Almost immediately she began preaching and talking about Jesus every chance she got. She took her children to church regularly and became very involved in the African Methodist Episcopal (A.M.E.) church. In fact, one member of the Dumont family described Bell during this time as a "roaring Methodist."[4]

After many years in New York City, Bell felt God leading her to become an itinerant evangelist, going wherever He led her and depending on His providence to care for her needs. She already had a reputation as a powerful, forceful, and convincing preacher in her church; now God wanted her to step out and preach to others.

Bell felt that the name given her as a slave was inappropriate for a person setting out on a new life as God's pilgrim, so she asked God to give her a new name. She recalled a verse from Psalm 39: "Hear my prayer, O Lord, and give ear unto my cry...for I am a stranger with Thee, and a sojourner, as all my fathers were" (Ps. 39:12 KJV). She realized that "Sojourner" was a good name for someone who wandered up and down the land, showing the people their sins.[5] She realized also that only slaves had no last name, so she wanted a last name. Again remembering Scripture, she was inspired by Jesus' words, "And ye shall know the truth, and the truth shall make you free" (Jn. 8:32 KJV). Bell had only one master—God—and His name was Truth. She became Sojourner Truth.[6]

Years later, she explained her name change to Harriet Beecher Stowe:

> When I left the house of bondage, I left everything behind. I wa'nt goin' to keep nothin' of Egypt on me, an so I went to the Lord an' asked Him to give me a new name. And the Lord gave me Sojourner, because I was to travel up an' down the land, showin' the people their sins, an' bein' a sign unto them. Afterwards I told the Lord I wanted another name, 'cause everybody else had two names; and the Lord gave me Truth, because I was to declare the truth to the people.[7]

Rise of an Activist

Following God's instruction to "Go east," Sojourner headed across Long Island, preaching in the farms and villages along the way. She had no trouble gathering a crowd because a black woman itinerant preacher was somewhat of an oddity at the time. Those who did come to hear Sojourner were moved mightily by the hymns she sang and by the persuasive power of her message and personality. Before long, her reputation spread until she was so popular that whenever she showed up at a religious gathering in a town or village, people flocked to hear her. Her message focused on the love and mercy of God and on the evils of slavery, which quickly became the central focus of her ministry.

Sojourner's travels eventually brought her to Northampton, Massachusetts, where she stayed for a while at a cooperative community, the Northampton Association of Education and Industry. The community, which operated a silkworm farm and made silk, was run by Samuel L. Hill, an ex-Quaker, and George Benson. Both men were ardent supporters of the abolition of slavery, and Benson was the brother-in-law of William Lloyd Garrison, who was considered by many to be the leader of the anti-slavery movement.[8]

Sojourner's stay at Northampton brought her into contact with many of the prominent abolitionist leaders of the day: Garrison,

Sojourner Truth: "Ain't I a Woman?"

Wendell Phillips, Park Pillsbury, David Ruggles, and Frederick Douglass. Because of the forcefulness of her personality and her captivating hold on audiences, Sojourner was recruited by the abolitionists and began to travel with some of them, lecturing in many different towns and villages. Also during her stay at Northampton, Sojourner heard lecturers advocating equal political and legal rights for women. This call for women's freedom struck a responsive chord in Sojourner's heart, and she became an active supporter and lecturer for women's rights. These were natural responses for her because she was black and a woman in a society that placed severe restrictions on both blacks and females.[9]

Where did Sojourner Truth get the courage to be so bold as a black woman in such a repressive society? She was absolutely convinced that God would protect her as she tried to follow His instructions and do His will. Once, before a meeting, trouble was anticipated. Her friends encouraged her to carry a pistol, but Sojourner responded, "I carry no weapon; the Lord will preserve me without weapons. I feel safe even in the midst of my enemies; for the truth is powerful and will prevail."[10] God honored her faith. Even though she suffered much ridicule and abuse, at times being shouted down, spat upon, and even stoned, she never gave up, never lost faith, never wavered in courage, and was never seriously injured.

The focus of Sojourner's abolitionist message was different from that of others. Whereas most abolitionists stressed the plight of the slaves, Sojourner stressed the plight of the slave owners, who, she warned, would end up in hell if they did not change. This was not speech tinged with hatred, but rather Christ-like concern. At a meeting in Syracuse, New York, in 1850, she shared the podium with a popular abolitionist speaker named George Thompson. Some of the audience who had come to hear Thompson were angry when Sojourner rose to speak first. She demonstrated her remarkable ability to calm a crowd and speak right to their hearts when she said to them, "I'll tell you what Thompson is going to say

65

to you. He is going to argue that the poor Negroes ought to be out of slavery and in the heavenly state of freedom. But, children, I'm against slavery because I want to keep the white folks who hold slaves from getting sent to hell."[11]

On another occasion when the radical abolitionist Henry C. Wright bitterly attacked churches that cooperated with slavery, calling them "so-called churches," Sojourner disagreed. She said, "We ought to be like Christ. He said, 'Father, forgive them, they know not what they do.' If we want to lead the people, we must not be out of their sight."[12]

Advocate for Women

Sojourner Truth is remembered most for an extemporaneous speech she gave at a convention on women's rights held in Akron, Ohio, in 1851. Her attendance at the convention was unexpected. She had been lecturing in another Ohio town when she heard of the meeting in Akron. When she arrived, the church hosting the convention was already full. Amid whispers and murmurs Sojourner walked proudly to the front and sat down on one of the steps leading to the pulpit. No other seats were available.

The others attending the conference had mixed reactions to Sojourner's presence. Some were eager to hear her speak, while others, fearing that her involvement with the abolitionist movement would lead to negative publicity for the Akron conference, appealed to Mrs. Frances Gage, the convener of the conference, to not let Sojourner speak.

During the first day of the conference Sojourner made no attempt to speak. She simply sat quietly, listening to the different speakers. Both sides of the issue were debated. Most of those in attendance favored equal rights for women but there was a significant number of people who did not. Many of these were members of the clergy who sought to attack the movement on biblical grounds.

Sojourner Truth: "Ain't I a Woman?"

On the second day of the conference, Sojourner listened as a succession of ministers spoke. One claimed that men deserved greater rights and privileges than women because men were more intelligent than women. Another claimed that men should rule over women because Christ was a man. A third said that women had a lower status because Eve had committed the original sin. Still another minister said that women were inferior to men because they were weaker and had to be helped into carriages and over mud puddles and the like.

After this verbal barrage the room was silent. In those days there were few women who dared to speak up in a public meeting, particularly in the face of a strong male presence. Sojourner, however, had no such timidity. She stood up and moved to the podium, looking at Mrs. Gage for permission to speak. There were hisses and murmurs from those in the audience who did not want to hear her. Mrs. Gage hesitated for a few moments, then introduced the speaker by saying simply, "Sojourner Truth."

Sojourner calmed her audience by very slowly and deliberately removing her bonnet and waiting for a few moments before beginning. She addressed point by point the arguments presented by the ministers who had preceded her:

Dat man ober dar say dat womin needs to be helped into carriages, and lifted ober ditches, and to hab de best place everywhar. Nobody eber helps me into carriages, or ober mud-puddles, or gibs me any best place! And ain't I a woman? Look at me! Look at my arm! I have ploughed, and planted, and gathered into barns, and no man could head me! And ain't I a woman? I could work as much and eat as much as a man—when I could get it—and bear de lash as well! And ain't I a woman? I have borne...chilern, and seen 'em mos' all sold off to slavery, and when I cried out with my mother's grief, none but Jesus heard me! And ain't I a woman?[13]

Regarding the claim that men are more intelligent than women, Sojourner said, "What's intellect got to do wid womin's rights or black folks' rights? If my cup won't hold but a pint, and yours holds a quart, wouldn't you be mean not to let me have my little half-measure full?"[14]

To the minister who claimed women's inferiority because Christ was a man Sojourner gave this rebuke: "Whar did your Christ come from? From God and a woman! Man had nothin' to do wid Him."[15]

Concerning Eve's position as the first sinner and thus relegating women to a lower position than men, Sojourner said, "If de fust woman God ever made was strong enough to turn de world upside down all alone, dese women togedder ought to be able to turn it back, and get it right side up again! And now dey is askin' to do it, de men better let 'em. Bleeged to ye for hearin' on me, and now ole Sojourner han't got nothin' more to say."[16]

Loud cheers and long applause followed Sojourner's spontaneous speech. It was the turning point of the conference, winning the day for the supporters of women's rights.

Sojourner's Legacy

Sojourner Truth approached life with dignity, courage, and deep commitment to the God who had shown His love to her in such a profound way. She remained a staunch advocate for women's rights and the abolition of slavery. Like many others she rejoiced at President Lincoln's signing of the Emancipation Proclamation in 1863. After the Civil War she worked tirelessly for the betterment and advancement of her race.

We can take courage from the life of Sojourner Truth because, by God's help and direction, she overcame obstacles and met challenges greater than any that most of us will ever face. She was black, female, and illiterate; yet she captivated and moved countless numbers of white, educated, and highly refined people. She conquered hatred and bitterness in her own heart and returned love and compassion to everyone, even to those who hated her and had abused her.

Sojourner's motivation for everything that she did was her love for God and His love shed abroad in her heart. A courageous person by nature, she also was endowed with a supernatural courage from beyond herself that made her fearless in the face of opposition. When she gave herself to the Lord, she gave herself completely, and He used her accordingly.

Sojourner Truth spent more than 50 years on the front lines, and God sustained her and guided her steps. He never changes in nature, purpose, or character. As He guided and sustained Sojourner Truth, so He will guide and sustain you as you trust Him and follow Him. The same courage He gave to her He will give to you. Believe Him and claim His promise!

A contemporary of Sojourner Truth, Harriet Tubman also knew and walked in the divine guidance of her Lord and Savior. Perhaps you too will hear a call from God as you read the following pages of her story.

Endnotes

1. W. Terry Whalin, *Sojourner Truth: American Abolitionist* (Uhrichsville, OH: Barbour Publishing, Inc., 1997), 195.
2. Arthur Huff Fauset, *Sojourner Truth, God's Faithful Pilgrim* (New York: Russell & Russell, 1971), 57-63.
3. Harriet Beecher Stowe, "Sojourner Truth, The Libyan Sibyl," *Atlantic Monthly 11* (April 1863), 473-481. 9 SEP 1998 <http://www.kn.pacbell.com/wired/BHM/sojourner_truth. txt>, 4.
4. Whalin, *Sojourner Truth*, 55-56.
5. Victoria Ortiz, *Sojourner Truth, A Self-Made Woman* (Philadelphia, PA: J.B. Lippincott Company, 1974), 44.
6. Whalin, *Sojourner Truth*, 87.

7. Stowe, "Sojourner Truth," 7.
8. Whalin, *Sojourner Truth*, 94.
9. Whalin, *Sojourner Truth*, 101.
10. Whalin, *Sojourner Truth*, 152.
11. Ortiz, *Sojourner Truth*, 62.
12. Whalin, *Sojourner Truth*, 118.
13. Frances D. Gage as quoted in Elizabeth Cady Stanton, Susan B. Anthony, and Matilda Joslyn Gage, eds., *History of Woman Suffrage*, Vol. 1 (Reprinted New York: Arno Press, 1969). 15 February 1999 <http://blackhistory.eb.com/blackhistory/pri/q00160.html>, 2.
14. "Ain't I a Woman?" *Digital Sojourn.* 17 April 1998 <http://www.digitalsojourn.org/speech.html>.
15. Stanton, *History*, 2.
16. Stanton, *History*, 2.

Chapter 6

Harriet Tubman: Go Down, Moses

One day in April 1860, a fugitive slave named Charles Nalle was captured in Troy, New York. According to the Fugitive Slave Law of 1850, it was legal to capture runaway slaves found in the North and return them to their owners in the South. Nalle had escaped from a Virginia plantation in 1858 and joined his wife and children, who had been set free earlier, in Pennsylvania. They later moved to Troy where Charles had found work. Charles and his wife were "octoroons"—one-eighth black and seven-eighths white— and therefore looked completely white. Nevertheless, a man in Troy suspected Charles of being a runaway and had him arrested.

Charles was held in the city courthouse, which was soon surrounded by angry protesters from the strongly anti-slavery town. The officials were hesitant to bring Nalle down through the crowd to a waiting wagon. Then an old black woman walked into the courthouse. Seeing a young boy nearby, she told him to run outside and yell "Fire, fire!" as loudly as he could. In the ensuing chaos on the streets, the officials saw their chance and brought Charles downstairs. The old woman yelled through a window to the crowd. "Don't let them take him! Don't let them take him!" Then she attacked the nearest officer holding Nalle, knocking him down. Grabbing Nalle by the arm, she pulled him out of the courthouse and into the midst of the crowd.[1]

Nalle was transported by the crowd down to the river where a rowboat took him across. His mysterious rescuer followed in a ferry boat. On the other side a policeman saw Nalle's handcuffs and detained him. He was taken to a nearby house. The old black woman and other rescuers promptly stormed the house. Two of them were wounded by police gunfire, but the woman and the others succeeded in rescuing Nalle once again. By chance, a man was passing by in a wagon. Upon finding out what was happening, he immediately relinquished his wagon. Nalle was put aboard with a few of his supporters and escaped to Schenectady, New York, and subsequently to Canada.[2]

The "old" black woman who so boldly secured Charles Nalle's rescue was in fact 40-year-old Harriet Tubman, herself a runaway slave with a heavy price on her head. Since her own escape from a Maryland plantation 11 years earlier, Harriet had repeatedly put her life on the line by returning to the South to lead many fellow slaves to freedom. On that day in Troy, Harriet was visiting a cousin and heard about Nalle's capture. Although the broad daylight and public nature of the rescue were not typical of Harriet's methods, the bold action and unshakable courage were certainly characteristic of her.

Liberty or Death

Harriet's commitment to freedom—for herself as well as for others—was forged by two major influences in her life. The first of these was slavery itself. Beginning as a young child of six, Harriet was hired out by her owner to work for a succession of different people, many of whom abused her terribly. Very early she learned to endure the lash of the whip on her back and was often beaten severely for minor offenses—sometimes for no reason at all. As

Harriet grew older the conviction grew in her heart that everyone deserved to be free. Slavery was unjust. Freedom was worth any price.

The second influence in the development of Harriet's character was her faith. Along with many other slaves, Harriet and her family found strength and comfort in the community they shared together. Sundays afforded them the opportunity to gather for informal worship services. They listened to Bible stories, sang songs inspired by those stories, and prayed. The slaves found hope and encouragement in the experiences of biblical characters such as Job, Joseph, Noah, Paul, Abraham, and Moses. Jesus was especially dear to them because He had suffered the way they suffered.[3]

By the time Harriet reached adulthood her hatred of slavery had made her determined to be free at any cost, while her faith in God had instilled in her a confidence in her success and a fearlessness regarding her own personal safety. Those who saw Harriet in action during her years of personally leading slaves to freedom were impressed by the fact that she displayed absolutely no fear for herself while taking every care to protect the runaways she was responsible for. She believed implicitly that God was directing her steps and protecting her, and that she would be taken only when and if God willed it. As Harriet herself expressed it to friends years later, "There are two things I have a right to, liberty or death. If I can't have one, I will have the other. For no man will take me alive. I will fight for my liberty as long as my strength lasts, and when the time comes for me to go, the Lord will let them take me."[4]

When she was 25, Harriet married John Tubman, a free black. John had been born free and therefore had never known what slavery was like. He had a difficult time understanding Harriet's burning desire to be free. When Harriet made the decision to run away, she could not persuade John to come north with her. She determined to go alone.

Five years after her marriage Harriet knew that the time had come to make her escape. She was prompted to act by the rumor and fear that she was about to be "sold South"—sold to another master in the deep South where escape was much less likely and conditions for slaves much worse than in Maryland. Harriet knew it was now or never. Carrying a slip of paper bearing the name of someone who would help her, Harriet took off through the woods one night. The paper had been given to her by a Quaker woman who had also given Harriet directions for finding the house where this person lived.

Harriet found the house and was welcomed and sheltered during the day hours. Then in the night she was taken to the edge of town and given directions for finding the next place of shelter. Harriet was now a "passenger" on the "Underground Railroad" that she had heard about since her childhood. Gradually over many days, traveling at night and taking shelter by day, Harriet covered more than 90 miles, finally reaching Wilmington, Delaware. She took shelter with a Quaker named Thomas Garrett, who ran a shoe store. He allowed Harriet to rest for a day and gave her new shoes to replace her worn-out ones. That night he took her to the road north and told her to watch for the wooden sign that would mark the state line between Delaware and Pennsylvania.

The moment she walked across the state line into Pennsylvania, Harriet was overwhelmed with joy. For the first time in her life she was free! Years later she described the feeling: "I looked at my hands to see if I was the same person now I was free. Dere was such a glory trou de trees and ober de fields, and I felt like I was in heaven."[5]

The "Moses" of Her People

Harriet made her way to Philadelphia where she found work as a cook and maid at a hotel. She also found an inexpensive place to rent and began enjoying life as a free woman. Her heart was burdened, however, at the thought of her family—her brothers and sisters and her aging parents—still in bondage. She resolved within herself that with the Lord's help she would see all of them to freedom.

Before long she became involved with the Philadelphia Vigilance Committee, a branch of the Underground Railroad. The Committee helped runaway slaves in every way possible—from organizing escapes to helping escapees adjust to freedom. In 1850 the Committee learned that Harriet's sister Mary Ann and her family wanted to escape. They were in danger of being sold South. The Committee had made arrangements to get them as far as Baltimore, but they needed someone to bring them the rest of the way. Without a moment's hesitation Harriet said she would go.

Some of Harriet's friends were worried that she might be caught if she went back into Maryland, but Harriet herself had no such fear. She traveled to Baltimore where she waited until her sister, brother-in-law, and their children arrived. Harriet hid them for several days and then successfully brought them to Philadelphia.

This was the first of a total of 19 trips into Maryland that Harriet made over the decade before the Civil War. She is credited with personally leading more than 300 slaves to freedom, including, as she had promised, her parents and all her brothers and sisters and their families. What is even more remarkable is that she never lost a single one. Every slave who followed Harriet was delivered safely to freedom in the North. Harriet was bold, fearless, creative, cunning, and, when necessary, severe. Most of the runaways who followed her trusted her absolutely. Occasionally one or two would give in to fear and want to turn back. Whenever this happened, Harriet would pull a pistol from beneath her skirt and promise to shoot anyone who turned back. Any runaways who returned home would be tortured into revealing information about the Underground Railroad, possibly endangering many lives. There was too much at stake. Harriet made it clear that there was no turning back.

Time after time Harriet ventured into Maryland on her missions of freedom. Her reputation spread far and wide among the slaves, who called her the "Moses" of her people, as well as among the slave-holders who put a $40,000 price on her head. Despite this she labored on fearlessly, working hard and giving God the credit: "Jes' so long as he wanted to use me, he would take keer of me, an' when he didn't want me no longer, I was ready to go; I always tole him, 'I'm gwine to hole steady onto you, an' you've got to see me trou.'"[6]

Harriet talked to God constantly, and He spoke to her in answer to her prayers and through dreams and visions. As a child of 13 Harriet had been severely injured when a plantation overseer, trying to stop a fleeing slave, had thrown an iron weight at him. Instead of hitting the man, the weight hit Harriet squarely on the forehead, crushing in the front of her skull. For weeks she lingered at the point of death, in and out of consciousness. It took her months to recover. After this, she began to have vivid, even prophetic, dreams. For the rest of her life Harriet also suffered periodic attacks of narcolepsy—she would suddenly fall asleep in the middle of whatever she was saying or doing, sleep for a few minutes, then wake up, picking up where she had left off as though nothing had happened.

In 1851 Harriet made a trip into Maryland to lead James, her oldest brother, to freedom. James and two friends left with Harriet in the middle of the night. Unfortunately, their escape was discovered very early and they were quickly pursued by bloodhounds and men on horseback. It seemed that only a miracle could save them. As they ran through the woods, Harriet heard a voice inside warning her of danger ahead. She turned to the left and the men followed, only to find their way blocked by a river. Harriet's voice told her to cross the river. Without hesitation she plunged in and began wading to the other side. The water rose to her waist, then to her shoulders, then to her chin. Then it got shallower again until she reached the other side. The three men with her had hesitated

76

at first, then plunged in after her with their pursuers close behind them in the woods.

The four of them soon came to a cabin where a family of free blacks lived. There they received shelter and food. Later Harriet learned that just ahead of them, before they had crossed the river, posters had been placed advertising rewards for their capture and officers had been waiting for them.[7] Had Harriet not listened to the voice inside her, she and her charges would surely have been captured. This is just one example of the divine guidance and providence that sustained Harriet and helped her succeed against incredible odds.

Harriet and those with her made it safely to the Wilmington, Delaware, home of Thomas Garrett, the Quaker who had originally helped Harriet during her own escape. Garrett was quite impressed with Harriet, and particularly by her confidence in and dependence upon God. He said of her:

> ...For in truth I never met with any person, of any color, who had more confidence in the voice of God, as spoken direct to her soul....She talked with God, and he talked with her every day of her life....She felt no more fear of being arrested by her former master, or any other person, when in his immediate neighborhood, than she did in the State of New York, or Canada, for she said she never ventured [except] where God sent her, and her faith in the Supreme Power was great.[8]

Harriet's Legacy

Harriet settled with her parents in Auburn, New York, in 1857 and made her last trip into Maryland in November 1860, just a few months before the Civil War began. During the war she was recruited as a spy and a scout for the Union and successfully carried out several information-gathering missions behind Confederate lines. She also served as a nurse, gaining quite a reputation as a healer. Harriet had learned from her father many native remedies from herbs and tree roots, and the medicines she made from these often worked better than the more modern kinds that the doctors used.

After the war she returned to Auburn; married Nelson Davis, a black soldier she had met during the war; and became involved in the women's suffrage movement. She always opened her home to any who were in need—particularly blacks—and was so generous with what resources she had that she struggled all her life to have enough money for her own needs. In her later years she established on her property a home for aged and impoverished blacks. Eventually, Harriet deeded the property and the home to the AME Zion Church, with which she was actively involved during her years in Auburn. Harriet Tubman died in Auburn on March 10, 1913, greatly admired and respected for her courage, service, and high Christian and moral character. She was given a military funeral.

Harriet Tubman's life is a testimony to what a person can do who learns to listen to God's voice and obey without question. Because she trusted not in herself but in Him, she found His courage, strength, wisdom, insight, and protection available to her. Those same resources are ours as well if we will trust God and not depend on ourselves.

Let's also listen and obey the Spirit's voice. Who knows? Maybe you too will be added to the hall of heroes and heroines of courage as God enables you to proclaim, "Let My people go!"

Pioneers always blaze a trail for others to later walk. Let's next gaze at the life of Jesus exhibited through one of the most passionate and powerful apostolic evangelists who ever lived: Aimee Semple McPherson.

Endnotes

1. Ann Petry, *Harriet Tubman: Conductor on the Underground Railroad* (New York: Thomas Y. Crowell, 1955), 214-217.

2. Judy Carlson, *Harriet Tubman: Call to Freedom* (New York: Fawcett Columbine, 1989), 79-81.
3. Carlson, *Harriet Tubman*, 29.
4. Carlson, *Harriet Tubman*, 4.
5. Russell Smith, "Harriet Tubman: Moses of the Civil War." <http://www.camalott.com/~rssmith/Moses.html>.
6. Sarah Bradford, *Harriet Tubman, The Moses of Her People* (New York: Corinth, 1969), 61.
7. Bradford, *Harriet Tubman*, 49-51.
8. Bradford, *Harriet Tubman*, 83-84.

Chapter 7

Aimee Semple McPherson: Yesterday, Today, and Forever

It was a sight no one in Mount Forest, Ontario, had ever seen before: a slim, attractive young woman standing on a chair in the middle of the small town's main intersection. With her eyes closed and her arms raised, she said nothing and did not move. The crowd that quickly gathered around her was curious, amused, puzzled. Murmured questions were passed from one to another, receiving shrugged shoulders in reply. There were a few snickers.

For several minutes the young woman stood silent and motionless as the ever-growing crowd stared at her. Suddenly, she jumped off the chair, picked it up, and ran down the street, calling back to the crowd, "Follow me!" They did and she led them into a small mission church building where, after the doors were closed behind them, she preached Christ to them.

It was August 1915. The audience-gathering technique was a Salvation Army tactic known as a "Hallelujah run"; the meeting place was a tiny, struggling Pentecostal church named Victory Mission; and the energetic woman preacher was a 24-year-old evangelist named Aimee Semple McPherson. This day was a significant one for Aimee; until her death nearly 30 years later she never again had to work at gathering a crowd.[1]

One source of Aimee's tremendous appeal to the millions who flocked to her meetings over the years was that she never forgot who she was, a simple Canadian country farm girl. In fact, her story of how God called her from her simple origins to do the work of His Kingdom became a major theme in her preaching.

Another source of her popularity was her flair for the dramatic. Her style was different from that of anyone else. She developed early on the use of "illustrated sermons"—staged messages that eventually reached a complexity and quality equal to those of Hollywood films and professional theater.

The primary reason for her lasting appeal, however, was the sincerity and simplicity of her message. Aimee Semple McPherson was genuinely concerned about the spiritual condition of the people who came to hear her, and it showed in her actions. She preached a simple gospel centered around Hebrews 13:8: "Jesus Christ the same yesterday, and to day, and for ever" (KJV).

How did a simple Canadian farm girl rise up to become one of the most popular, prominent, and influential Christian evangelists of the twentieth century, even being referred to by many as "the female Billy Sunday"?

Humble Beginnings

Aimee Elizabeth Kennedy was born October 9, 1890, in Salford, Ontario, Canada, to James and Minnie Kennedy. Minnie was James's second wife and was 35 years his junior—younger than any of his children by his deceased first wife. Minnie was originally brought into the Kennedy home to care for James' first wife as she struggled with terminal illness. Later, James chose to marry his wife's nurse. It was a marriage of convenience: James needed a woman on the farm, and Minnie, an orphan who had been travel-ing with some Salvation Army officers, needed a home.[2]

Aimee's early life centered around the slow, seasonal cycles of the farm, the Methodist church of her father, and the Salvation Army of her mother. All these factors helped to shape Aimee's personality and character. Both Methodism and Salvationism were major influences in the later development of her spiritual attitudes and approach to ministry.

From an early age Aimee displayed a talent for public speaking; during her school years she won several medals. She was a bright student and by her teen years was in demand locally for parties, concerts, plays, and other types of entertainment. Popular, ener-getic, and fun-loving, Aimee brightened up whatever corner she was in.

One day on the way to a drama rehearsal in nearby Ingersoll, Aimee stopped in at a small Pentecostal mission. She had heard a little about the "Pentecostals," was curious, and wanted to observe for a few minutes. In spite of herself she was captivated by the handsome young visiting evangelist who spoke with a melodic Irish brogue. His name was Robert Semple. After only a few min-utes Aimee was hooked, not only by Robert, but by his message as well. Realizing her need to repent of her sins and come to Jesus, Aimee agonized for three days over the cost of following God, then threw herself heart and soul into her newfound faith.[3] For Aimee, once she had made her decision, there was no turning back, no halfway measures. It was all or nothing.

A Rocky Start

Before long romance blossomed between Aimee and Robert, and they married at Aimee's home in August 1908. The newlyweds embarked on evangelistic work together, spending about a year ministering alongside William Durham, a former Baptist and early Pentecostal leader in Chicago.

Answering the call for world evangelization that so many Pentecostals felt at the time, Robert and Aimee left Chicago in January 1910 to go to China as missionaries. They arrived in Hong Kong on June 1, 1910, and joined several other Pentecostal missionaries who were already there. Their excitement was short-lived, however. In August, after barely two months in China, both Robert and Aimee contracted severe cases of malaria. Aimee, eight months pregnant, recovered slowly, but Robert did not. On August 19, 1910, one week after their second anniversary, Robert died.

Sad, lonely, and confused, Aimee returned to the United States with her infant daughter Roberta and moved in with her mother Minnie, who was now living in New York City. Minnie had answered the call of Salvation Army work in New York, leaving her aged husband James on the farm in Salford. Aimee did some Salvation Army work for a few weeks but was increasingly restless. She took Roberta and went to Chicago to renew relationships with friends whom she and Robert had known there. A brief visit to her father in Salford followed. Aimee then went back to Chicago, hoping to settle and get involved in Pentecostal work there. Roberta's poor health intervened, however, and Aimee returned to New York City.

Early in 1911 Aimee met Harold McPherson. After several months of dating he proposed marriage and she accepted. Minnie disapproved, however, so Harold and Aimee eloped to Chicago where they were married in a civil ceremony. A church wedding followed a few weeks later. With this marriage to an American, Aimee became an American citizen.[4]

Unfortunately, the marriage was in trouble from the start. Harold wanted Aimee to focus on him and their relationship, but Aimee quickly became heavily involved once more with her Pentecostal friends and the activities and ministries she and Robert had worked in a couple of years before. During this time Aimee struggled with guilt over the feeling that she had abandoned the call of God that had once seemed so clear. She began to feel that she was being forced to make a decision between Harold and God. Even the birth of a son, Rolf, in March 1913, did not settle the domestic situation for Aimee and Harold. It took a severe health crisis for Aimee to decide her direction in life.

Late in 1913 Aimee fell ill and required surgery. She did not recover adequately and needed additional surgery. She resisted, apparently in the hope that God would heal her. An attack of appendicitis made her condition critical. Even after surgery she was not expected to live. While lying in a room set apart for the dying, Aimee heard a voice she believed to be God's saying, "NOW WILL YOU GO?" Recognizing that she had a choice either of entering eternity or entering the ministry, she yielded. Instantly her pain went away and she could breathe more easily. Within two weeks she was up and about.[5]

Harold did not understand Aimee's renewed commitment to God's call to full-time ministry. Aimee believed that God had spared her only because she had vowed to obey His call. She felt she had to follow God whether Harold did or not.

In late June 1915, while Harold was out of town, Aimee took her children and went to Salford. Leaving them with her father and her mother, who was visiting from New York, Aimee attended a camp meeting in a nearby town where she ministered powerfully, speaking in tongues and praying for people to receive the baptism of the Holy Spirit. Her career as an evangelist was off and running.[6]

Immediately after leaving with their children, Aimee had sent a telegram to Harold: "I have tried to walk your way and have failed. Won't you come now and walk my way? I am sure we will be happy."[7] After failing to persuade her to return through numerous letters and telegrams, Harold did show up for the meetings in Mount Forest, Ontario, where one night he received the baptism of the Holy Spirit. Following this, Aimee and Harold embarked together on a full-time evangelistic ministry, traveling up and down the eastern United States and holding meetings wherever they could. Harold was not really cut out for this kind of life, however, and they began to drift apart. Early in 1918 he and Aimee separated. They divorced in 1921.

San Diego, California, 1921

The end of her marriage to Harold was difficult personally for Aimee, but it enabled her to give single-minded devotion to her ministry. Once she began in earnest in 1915, her fame spread and her popularity grew. This remained true even later, despite her divorce. Everywhere she went she experienced overflow crowds and the apparent presence and power of God in her meetings and messages.

By 1919 Aimee and her children had settled in Los Angeles, California, the city that would be her home for the rest of her life and that she used as a base for her itinerant evangelism. She always called her house on Orange Grove Drive in Los Angeles, the "House That God Built," because the land, the house, its furnishings, and the landscaping—all just a half block away from a school for her children—had been donated to her by people attending her meetings.[8]

The year 1921 was one of remarkable meetings for Aimee, beginning in San Diego, California, in January. The meetings were held in the 3,000-seat Dreamland Arena, which very quickly proved inadequate to contain the crowds that turned out each day. Aimee conducted both preaching services and healing services, and the public response to both was phenomenal. Thousands had to be turned away every day, causing Aimee to institute a reservations system, giving free tickets and reserving half of the building for those who had not yet been able to attend a service.[9]

Unlike many other evangelists of the time who stressed "hellfire and brimstone," Aimee focused on a message of love and acceptance. This was undoubtedly one of the major reasons for her enormous appeal. Aimee's message was, in her own words, "the simple story of Jesus' love, and the outpoured Holy Spirit who has come to convict us of sin and draw us to the cross of Calvary, where, as we confess our sin, Jesus...cleanseth us from all unrighteousness."[10] She believed that the secret of her success was her emphasis on Christ.

Originally scheduled for two weeks, the meetings were extended twice. Even after five weeks there was no ebb in the tide of people coming for prayer, especially prayer for healing. Aimee tried at first to pray personally for as many as possible, but the demand was too great. In response to the overwhelming need, two outdoor healing services were scheduled in Balboa Park. San Diego police augmented by U.S. Marines and U.S. Army personnel handled traffic and crowd control. A Salvation Army band, an orchestra, and a large combined choir were on hand. Aimee also depended on a group of local ministers present to assist in anointing the sick with oil, the laying on of hands, and praying for healing.[11] As many as 30,000 people crowded into the park. The service began at 10:30 in the morning and by nightfall the sick were still coming.

The January 1921 meetings in San Diego are just one example of the enormous popularity and influence that Aimee Semple McPherson enjoyed throughout her ministry, particularly in the early years.

The Foursquare Gospel

On January 1, 1923, Aimee Semple McPherson dedicated the Angelus Temple, the church building in Los Angeles that would become the hub of the wide-ranging ministries of her Echo Park Evangelistic Association. The full, or official, name of the church was the International Church of the Foursquare Gospel. The name "foursquare" referred to a four-point theme or emphasis that had become the doctrinal core of Aimee's preaching by the summer of 1922. It clearly illustrated the Christ-centered focus of her message: Jesus Christ as Savior, Healer, Baptizer in the Holy Spirit, and coming King.[12]

From the outset, Angelus Temple was one of the largest churches in Los Angeles. Its 5,300-seat sanctuary was filled to capacity regularly. The large platform area was built on hydraulic pistons so it could be raised or lowered to accommodate the needs of Aimee's illustrated sermons, which were an ever-popular feature of the Temple's Sunday night service. A full schedule of services of different types and for different age groups kept the church open seven days a week. Her message was so simple and straightforward, her style so warm, her methods so innovative, that she attracted a wide and diverse audience: Hollywood actors and actresses, politicians, common folk, African Americans, and even the Ku Klux Klan.

The various ministries of the Temple have always been very practical in focus, seeking to meet human needs in any form. The Temple commissary, which began operation in 1923, provided for the needs of thousands of poor and destitute people in the Los Angeles area. Other ministries extended help to women in trouble, alcoholics, prostitutes, and the uneducated. The Angelus Temple Prayer Tower also began in 1923, receiving and praying for thousands of requests and needs. From its beginning and for decades after Aimee's death, the Prayer Tower operated around the clock, 24 hours a day, every day of the year.

Each of these ministries were reflections of the heart of the woman who inspired them. Aimee genuinely loved people. She reached out personally to them wherever she went, often laboring far into the night to minister to them. People everywhere responded to and loved her for her compassion. Her heart for people also made her bold. She did not hesitate to go into a city's "red-light district" to talk with the prostitutes, to love them and share Jesus with them, and to invite them to her meetings. In San Diego in 1921 Aimee appeared between rounds at a boxing match to challenge those attending to find the "worst sinner in the city" and bring that person with them to the meeting the next night, where she promised to "go into the ring for Jesus."[13]

Aimee had a pioneering spirit and a vision for the future. This is revealed by the fact that in February 1924, radio station KFSG began broadcasting, making Angelus Temple one of the first churches in the country to own and operate its own radio transmission facility. Aimee Semple McPherson was also the first woman in America to own a radio broadcasting license and was one of the first women to preach over the radio.

Another sign of her far-reaching vision was her establishment of a training institute for ministers and other Christian workers. The institute was named L.I.F.E.: the Lighthouse of International Foursquare Evangelism. Through the years, this school has trained thousands of people for Christian ministry.

Aimee's Legacy

When Aimee Semple McPherson died on September 27, 1944, she left behind a remarkable record of accomplishments. The denomination she founded, the International Church of the Foursquare Gospel, still flourishes today with hundreds of churches and thousands of members worldwide. The Angelus Temple in Los Angeles still serves as the headquarters for the denomination and still conducts services to capacity crowds.

Aimee was the most well-known and popular evangelist of her day. By all accounts, she was very effective in reaching people with the gospel. During her life she personally baptized over 100,000 people. Although she is known by many for her healing ministry, her first priority was evangelism: winning people to saving faith in Jesus Christ. Healing was a vital part of what she called "full-gospel evangelism," but preaching Christ to save sinners was foremost. Although she was a Pentecostal, she de-emphasized many of the more controversial aspects and manifestations. She did not prohibit them, but she never allowed anything to get out of control.

Because of this and because of her infectious personality, Aimee's ministry enjoyed widespread interdenominational support. At one time or another she held ministerial credentials from the Assemblies of God, a Methodist exhorter's license, and a Baptist preaching license.

Aimee Semple McPherson was a woman of courage. She overcame the grief and trauma of early widowhood and the stigma of two divorces (one from a later, third marriage), and built a powerful and effective ministry. In a society that still placed significant social and public restrictions on women, Aimee prevailed against significant odds: prejudice against women ministers, the belief that women were not capable of succeeding without male guidance, and the belief that women did not have the ability to head large "business" organizations.

She was not afraid to speak the truth even against powerful people. One evening service at Angelus Temple was attended by hundreds of white-robed Ku Klux Klansmen. Aimee pulled no punches, saying to them plainly:

> You men who pride yourselves on patriotism, you men who have pledged yourselves to make America free for white Christianity, listen to me! Ask yourselves how is it possible to pretend to worship one of the greatest Jews who ever lived, Jesus Christ, and then to despise all living Jews? I say unto you as our Master said, "Judge not, that ye be not judged."[14]

Aimee even overcame the notorious scandal regarding her six-week disappearance in the spring of 1926. Her claim to have been kidnapped was never seriously investigated by the authorities, but their accusations of fraud, lying, and a sexual affair on her part fell to pieces under investigation because no evidence of any kind was uncovered to support them.

What was the secret of Aimee's success in ministry? Perhaps it can be summed up best in these words Aimee herself wrote in 1935:

Aimee Semple McPherson: Yesterday, Today, and Forever

O'er my head the lightning flashes,
Dark'ning clouds the heavens fill;
But I'm sheltered 'neath the cross-tree,
In the center of God's will;
There I fear no power of darkness,
For tho' man the body kill,
Yet my soul shall live forever
In the center of God's will.[15]

So far we've glanced at a variety of women who have carried difficult burdens and graces for their Lord. Zechariah the prophet said that Jerusalem is a heavy stone (see Zech. 12:3). Gaze now with me at a courageous soul who carried the cross of Christ by caring for the Jewish people. Consider the life of one appointed for Jersualem—Lydia Prince.

Endnotes

1. Edith L. Blumhofer, *Aimee Semple McPherson: Everybody's Sister* (Grand Rapids, MI: William B. Eerdmans Publishing Company, 1993), 108-109.
2. Don Taylor, "Aimee: A Short Biography," Liberty Harbor Foursquare Church, 1998, 1. <http://www.libertyharbor.org/aimec.htm>.
3. Daniel Mark Epstein, *Sister Aimee* (New York: Harcourt Brace Jovanovich, 1993), 47-50.
4. Blumhofer, *Aimee Semple McPherson*, 102-103.
5. Taylor, "Aimee," 4.
6. Taylor, "Aimee," 4.
7. Blumhofer, *Aimee Semple McPherson*, 107.
8. Lately Thomas, *Storming Heaven* (New York: William Morrow and Co., 1970), 20.
9. Blumhofer, *Aimee Semple McPherson*, 160.
10. Blumhofer, *Aimee Semple McPherson*, 159-160.
11. Blumhofer, *Aimee Semple McPherson*, 161.

12. Geoff Thurling, *Aimee Semple McPherson* (Brisbane, Australia: Anointed for Revival, 1995), 3. <http://www.pastornet.net.au/renewal/revival/mcpherso.htm>.
13. Epstein, *Sister Aimee*, 206-207.
14. Blumhofer, *Aimee Semple McPherson*, 277.
15. Blumhofer, *Aimee Semple McPherson*, 359.

Chapter 8

Lydia Prince:
The Peace of Jerusalem

By the time she was 36 years old, Lydia Christensen seemed to have it all: a good job, a good salary, a generous inheritance from her late father, a secure future, a growing relationship with a man who cared about her, and the respect of her colleagues in her chosen profession. What more could she want?

Lydia had already achieved the personal goals she had set for herself as a teacher. In addition to the standard certificates in history, geography, Danish, and English, she was one of the first teachers in Denmark to complete postgraduate study in domestic science. Now she was the director of domestic science in one of the largest and best-equipped schools in Denmark. Her department was used as a model for similar departments being established in other schools throughout the nation.[1] Lydia Christensen was at the height of her profession. What more could there be?

Like most Danish people of her generation, Lydia was a "good Lutheran"—baptized as an infant into the Danish state church, instructed as a child in its doctrines and beliefs, and as an adult settled in her religion, keeping it and God comfortably at arm's length. She had long since put away the childish things of religious devotion in favor of the sophisticated skepticism of the educated modern adult. Lydia had enough religion to be respectable but not enough to be inconvenienced. What more was needed?

By all normal standards of human measure Lydia should have been happy, satisfied, and on top of the world. Yet she wasn't. Something was missing.

The Search for Meaning

As the Christmas holiday of 1926 approached, Lydia Christensen was growing more and more restless with her life. She sensed that there must be more than she was experiencing but had no idea what it was. Born into a well-to-do Danish family, Lydia was the youngest of three children and the only one still unmarried. While at home with her family over the holiday break, Lydia discussed her yearnings with her mother. The elder woman felt that what Lydia was missing was a home and children of her own. Although Lydia couldn't explain how she felt, she knew it was deeper than that. Fumbling for the right words, Lydia told her mother, "If there was something special in life that another woman wouldn't do—even if it was difficult or dangerous—that's what I'd like to do!"[2]

After Christmas Lydia returned to her apartment in the Danish city of Korsor. She still had a week before school began again. Determined to find an answer to her inner restlessness, she gave her housekeeper the week off in order to spend the time completely alone.

Bypassing the books of philosophy and literature on her shelf, Lydia pulled down the Bible that she hadn't read since college days. She opened it to the Gospel of Matthew and began reading. The Beatitudes in chapter 5 spoke to her heart, especially the words, "Blessed are they which do hunger and thirst after righteousness:

94

for they shall be filled" (Mt. 5:6 KJV). Hungry and thirsty were just how she felt. Reading further, she was particularly arrested by Jesus' words in chapter 7:

> *Ask, and it shall be given you; seek, and ye shall find; knock, and it shall be opened unto you: for every one that asketh receiveth; and he that seeketh findeth; and to him that knocketh it shall be opened....Enter ye in at the strait gate: for wide is the gate, and broad is the way, that leadeth to destruction, and many there be which go in thereat: because strait is the gate, and narrow is the way, which leadeth unto life, and few there be that find it* (Matthew 7:7-8,13-14 KJV).

Lydia realized that if she were to find the way of peace and fulfillment, she had to enter through the gate. In order to find that gate she had to ask God to show her.[3] Kneeling in her living room Lydia prayed aloud, "O God—I do not understand—I do not understand—who is God, who is Jesus, who is the Holy Ghost...but if You will show me Jesus as a living reality, I will follow Him!"[4]

God answered Lydia's prayer. She saw a vision of Jesus standing before her, and for the first time in her life she knew—beyond doubt—that Jesus was real and that He was alive. Peace and joy flooded her heart. She developed a constant hunger for the Bible and for prayer. In response to her prayer, God delivered her instantly and completely from her smoking habit. A couple of weeks later, while reading in First John about joy, confession, cleansing, and forgiveness, Lydia was baptized in the Holy Spirit and spoke in tongues, something she had not consciously sought or prayed for because she knew very little about it.

Call to Jerusalem

During the same experience in which she spoke in tongues, Lydia received her second vision. She saw a barefooted woman in a long dress with an earthen jar balanced on her head. The woman was dancing slowly with her hands on her hips and chanting in a shrill voice. She was surrounded by a group of men who were clapping their hands in time to her song.[5] Lydia had no clue either to the woman's identity or nationality, yet she felt as if she were a part of the scene, as if she lived there or belonged there. It would be weeks before Lydia understood what it meant.

Lydia's conversion to Christ and baptism in the Holy Spirit created some difficulties for her professionally. Soon after these experiences she received water baptism by immersion and joined a small Pentecostal church. When word of this got around Lydia's school, she found herself ridiculed by her students behind her back and ostracized by her fellow teachers. There was even a movement begun among some of the faculty to force her to resign. She was called before her superiors to explain her actions. Although a formal review of her case by the Ministry of Education reaffirmed her right to her beliefs and her qualifications to teach, Lydia understood that her commitment to Christ had irreversibly changed many of her relationships.

During all of this Lydia was still trying to understand the meaning of her vision of the dancing woman and was seeking to learn God's will for her future. When her pastor told her about some churches in Sweden where people went to receive spiritual counsel, she decided to devote her summer vacation of 1927 to visiting those Pentecostal churches. One Sunday, at the largest Pentecostal church in Stockholm, Lydia listened to Dr. Bengt Karlsson, a Swedish missionary to the Congo, speak of his work there and his plans to build a small hospital in the jungle. Lydia felt the clear voice of God that she should help. Under the Spirit's leadership she gave $3,000—most of what remained from the inheritance she had received from her father—to help pay for the hospital.

While speaking with the Karlssons later Lydia shared her own experiences, particularly her questions regarding her vision. As she described it to them they helped her see that the dancing woman was dressed in the style of women in the Holy Land. From that moment Lydia began to sense a growing awareness that the

Lydia Prince: The Peace of Jerusalem

Holy Land, and especially Jerusalem, figured significantly in God's plans for her.

As her conviction grew that God was leading her to go to Jerusalem—for what reason she had no idea—Lydia had to face several serious questions. Was she prepared to truly be a woman of faith? Could she trust God to guide her steps and to provide for her every need no matter what it was? She had no inheritance left. If she resigned from her teaching position, she would have no income. Because of her Pentecostal ties no official Danish missionary society would appoint her. If she went to Jerusalem she would be leaving behind everything and everyone she had ever known and would be *totally* dependent upon God. Was she ready to make those sacrifices? Did she have the faith to take that step?

Two events helped Lydia resolve these questions. On December 4, 1927, during a special day of prayer at her church in Korsor, Lydia received another vision: the face of a baby girl staring up at her with black, solemn eyes. Lydia sensed that this child was a member of the growing family in Jerusalem—a family yet unknown to her—that she felt an increasing burden to pray for.

The second event was a specific answer to a specific prayer. Even though Lydia did not need money she prayed, "Please God, I want someone to give me five dollars before midnight tomorrow. If you will do this, then I will know that you can cause people to supply my needs even in Jerusalem."[6] At 9:30 p.m. the next night the school librarian, who was a Christian, stopped by and gave Lydia $5, saying that she had felt an unusual urging from God to do it. The next day, when she saw Lydia at school, the librarian gave her another $15, explaining that God had laid on her heart all along to give $20, but for some reason she had only given $5 the first time. Lydia realized that God had answered her prayer in the precise terms that she had requested! She no longer had any doubt that she was to go to Jerusalem.

During the spring school term of 1928 Lydia submitted her resignation, effective with the end of the term in July. Still not knowing *why* God wanted her in Jerusalem, Lydia began making preparations for her move. She sold her furniture, bought her steamship ticket, and arranged to be met in Palestine by a Swedish woman living in Jerusalem whose name Lydia had gotten from a missionary magazine.

Lydia sailed from Marseilles, France, on October 8, 1928, and arrived in Tel Aviv, Palestine, ten days later where she was met by the Swedish woman as arranged. They took a taxi to Jerusalem where Lydia spent the night with her new friend. The next day Lydia found a place of her own to rent. It was a small, sparsely furnished basement room in the home of a British missionary named Lorna Ratcliffe, and had a separate door and stairway leading to the street above. Lydia settled in with all her worldly possessions: two suitcases and a little more than a hundred dollars in cash. Now it was up to God to supply her needs and reveal to her why she was there.

Care for the Children

As the first few weeks went by Lydia's money dwindled and she was no closer to understanding why she was in Jerusalem. However, her conviction that God had led her there and had a purpose for her continued to grow. Her first impressions of the city of Jerusalem had been shocking, even frightening. Only ten years before at the end of the First World War in 1918, 13 centuries of Muslim rule in Palestine—four of them under the Ottoman Turks— had ended with the establishment of the British Mandate that now governed Palestine and the adjacent land of Transjordan. Relations between Arabs and Jews in the region—never very good to begin with—were strained even more under the new government. Tensions ran high.

Lydia Prince: The Peace of Jerusalem

Yet early on Lydia began to develop an unshakable love for the ancient city. She discovered two passages from the Psalms that opened her eyes to God's attitude toward Jerusalem:

If I forget thee, O Jerusalem, let my right hand forget her cunning. If I do not remember thee, let my tongue cleave to the roof of my mouth; if I prefer not Jerusalem above my chief joy (Psalm 137:5-6 KJV).[7]

Pray for the peace of Jerusalem: they shall prosper that love thee (Psalm 122:6 KJV).[8]

On Friday, December 28, 1928, a little more than two months after Lydia had arrived in Jerusalem, there was a knock on her door. Upon opening it Lydia met a man named Eliezer Cohen. Mr. Cohen and his wife had a baby daughter named Tikva who was dying. He asked Lydia if she would take Tikva. Lydia was mystified. Was this her mission in Jerusalem, to care for a sick and dying child? Besides, how had Mr. Cohen even heard of her?

At first Lydia put Mr. Cohen off, promising to pray about the situation. She then discovered why Mr. Cohen had come to her. An old, blind Arab woman named Nijmeh, who was a Christian and also lived with Lorna Ratcliffe, had met Tikva's mother earlier in the day and upon hearing of Tikva's condition, had recommended that they give the baby to Lydia. Nijmeh then explained that she had prayed for years for God to send someone to Jerusalem to care for children who had no home. Nijmeh believed that Lydia was that person.[9]

As Lydia prayed, she became more and more certain that God wanted her to take Tikva into her care. That very same day Lydia hurried over to the Cohen's house to pick her up. Tikva, though more than a year old, looked much younger because she was so thin and frail from illness. Her little body was burning with fever. Back at her basement room, Lydia placed Tikva in her wicker trunk and realized suddenly that Tikva was the baby she had seen in her vision during the church prayer meeting in Korsor! God had once again confirmed Lydia's calling to Jerusalem.

Lydia prayed for Tikva, claiming the promise found in James: "Is any sick among you? let him call for the elders of the church; and let them pray over him, anointing him with oil in the name of the Lord: and the prayer of faith shall save the sick, and the Lord shall raise him up" (Jas. 5:14-15a KJV). She took some olive oil and anointed Tikva's forehead. Lydia then went to Nijmeh, brought her to Tikva, and Nijmeh and Lydia prayed together for her. After a few hours Tikva's fever broke, and it became clear that she would recover.[10]

Lydia's Legacy

Lydia Christensen's life in Jerusalem is a wonderful example of a life truly lived by faith. She left behind all she had known and, like Abram centuries before, traveled to an unknown land simply by God's direction. Her circumstances demanded complete trust in God for the provision of every need. Time after time her resources ran low, only to be replenished by the unexpected arrival of letters or cards containing gifts of money. Some came from her mother, some from her former colleagues at the school in Korsor, some from other friends she knew. Some of the gifts were anonymous. Whatever the source, Lydia continually found her needs met by a bountiful and faithful God.

Lydia's absolute faith in God also gave her courage. She endured much hardship, privation, hunger, thirst, and even physical danger in a city and land torn by the centuries-old hostilities and strife between Jews and Arabs. She came to understand that her calling was not only to care for the homeless children of the city, but also to intercede in prayer; to pray continually for the "peace of Jerusalem."

Lydia lived in Jerusalem for more than 20 years, becoming "Mama" to scores of Arab and Jewish children she kept and loved

Lydia Prince: The Peace of Jerusalem

and cared for in her home. In 1945 she met Derek Prince, a British soldier stationed in Jerusalem. At this time Lydia's "family" consisted of eight girls: six Jewish, one Palestinian Arab, and one English.[11] Derek had become a Christian several years before in the early days of World War II. After the war he took his discharge in Jerusalem, entered full-time Christian ministry, and married Lydia. They remained in Jerusalem until 1948, witnessing the rebirth of the nation of Israel and enduring the new nation's war for independence.[12]

After leaving Israel, Lydia and Derek labored faithfully together through 30 years of marriage in Christian service that went from pastoring churches to a large and expanding international ministry. Lydia died suddenly of heart failure in 1975. She was in her mid-80's.

Lydia left behind a legacy of countless lives changed by the power of God and the living Christ. This is particularly true for those children who lived with her during her years in Jerusalem. Another, perhaps even more important legacy is her heart for Jerusalem and its people and her insight into God's plan for Israel, gained through many years of faithful prayer and loving service. This insight is best understood in Lydia's own words from a letter she wrote to her mother:

> You ask what you can do to help....We Christians have a debt that has gone unpaid for many centuries—to Israel and to Jerusalem. It is to them that we owe the Bible, the prophets, the apostles, the Savior Himself. For far too long we have forgotten this debt, but now the time has come for us to begin repaying it—and there are two ways that we can do this.
>
> First, we need to repent of our sins against Israel: at best, our lack of gratitude and concern; at worst, our open contempt and persecution.
>
> Then, out of true love and concern, we must pray as the psalmist tells us, "for the peace of Jerusalem," remembering that peace can only come to Jerusalem as Israel turns back to God.[13]

Perhaps you too are to be a burden bearer for Jesus, taking up your cross through missionary endeavors. Is He knocking on your heart to be an intercessor for Israel? My suggestion is to just say "Yes!" Surrender now to your appointment with the Jewish people by sharing the love of Yeshua. Say "yes"!

Another remarkable woman who lived on the front lines in a foreign country was Bertha Smith. Come with me as we observe Bertha's love for her Lord in the land of China....

Endnotes

1. Lydia and Derek Prince, *Appointment in Jerusalem* (Grand Rapids, MI: Chosen Books, 1975), 21. Used by permission. Derek Prince Ministries-International, P.O. Box 19501, Charlotte, NC 28219-5901.
2. Prince, *Appointment in Jerusalem*, 30.
3. Prince, *Appointment in Jerusalem*, 31-33.
4. Prince, *Appointment in Jerusalem*, 33.
5. Prince, *Appointment in Jerusalem*, 45-46.
6. Prince, *Appointment in Jerusalem*, 71.
7. Prince, *Appointment in Jerusalem*, 102.
8. Prince, *Appointment in Jerusalem*, 107.
9. Prince, *Appointment in Jerusalem*, 119.
10. Prince, *Appointment in Jerusalem*, 123-125.
11. Ruth Prince, "Derek Prince, His life, his work: Marriage and Ministry." 1995. 17 NOV 1998 <http://www.derekprince.com/dpmus/index.htm>.
12. Ruth Prince, "Derek Prince."
13. Prince, *Appointment in Jerusalem*, 174.

Chapter 9

Bertha Smith:
Walking in the Spirit

For two years Bertha had endured the buzzing in her ears. Although it was not constant, it was always irritating. Usually it would start in one ear and then move to the other. A specialist had diagnosed her condition as a degenerative "growing in" of her eardrums, a condition for which there was no cure. He had told Bertha that she would eventually go deaf. During the two years since the diagnosis Bertha had prayed daily for God to heal her ears, but nothing had happened.

At that time Bertha was the only Baptist missionary in the town of Tsining in the Shantung province of China. The church there had no pastor so Bertha, although she did not believe in women preachers, had taken up that responsibility out of necessity. A Chinese pastor from a large church in another Chinese city was invited to preach for a week in Bertha's church in Tsining. Pastor Fan Wei Ming had a reputation for praying for the sick, so on his first day in Tsining Bertha asked him to pray for healing for her ears. He put her off until later in the week.

The preaching theme for the week was personal holiness for Christians. Pastor Fan preached about the Feast of Unleavened Bread, urging all who heard to search their hearts for any leaven (sin) that was there. During this week Bertha became increasingly convinced by the Holy Spirit that she was going to be healed. The Spirit also led her into a deep awareness of the leaven in her own heart, particularly how she had used her ears to sin, always craving the compliments of others and the praise of men. Her conviction was so strong that for a time she could not eat or sleep. She confessed her sin to the Lord and committed her ears and her all to Him for cleansing.

On the last Sunday of the meetings several people gathered in Bertha's living room for prayer. Pastor Fan asked Bertha if she still wanted prayer for her ears. When she said that she did, they read from the Book of Exodus: "And the Lord said unto him, Who hath made man's mouth? or who maketh the dumb, or deaf, or the seeing, or the blind? have not I the Lord?" (Ex. 4:11 KJV) As they read, Bertha felt a physical sensation on each side of her face, as if a tight tendon was being loosed. Pastor Fan read from chapter 5 of James and then prayed.

Although Bertha knew in her spirit that she would be healed, healing did not come immediately. The buzzing continued, this time with a painful aching that became almost unbearable.[1] After a month of this aching, Bertha prayed, "Lord, you know that these ears are not mine! They were definitely given over to you, and since they are yours, they cannot hurt unless you let them hurt. Now if you do, it will be for some purpose and you will enable me to stand it, I know."[2] Within two weeks the pain and buzzing were completely gone. Two years later when Bertha was in the United States on furlough, a physical examination confirmed that her eardrums were in perfect condition with no evidence that there had ever been a problem.[3]

Bertha Smith: Walking in the Spirit

Called to China

Bertha's healing occurred in 1935 and is just one of many remarkable events in the life of a remarkable woman who lived in revival for 70 years. For nearly 42 years she gave herself to China as a missionary, witnessing and participating in one of the greatest revivals in history as it swept across China in the 1920's and 1930's. Retiring in 1958 at the age of 70, Bertha returned to the United States where she had another ministry of almost 30 years, awakening American Christians to their need for revival and inspiring them to pray for an awakening in the land.[4]

Olive Bertha Smith was appointed as a missionary to China by the Foreign Mission Board of the Southern Baptist Convention on July 3, 1917.[5] She was 28 years old. Her life since her conversion to Christ in 1905 had been marked by several deepening experiences in her walk with the Lord. The first came in 1907 when, during a revival service in her hometown of Cowpens, South Carolina, Bertha surrendered herself completely to the Lordship of Jesus Christ for anything that He might choose for her. She determined that nothing would be too much for Him to ask of her.[6] At this time she received her first "in-filling" of the Holy Spirit. As Bertha understood it, both then and to a greater degree later, being filled with the Holy Spirit was meant to be a continual and repeated experience for the Christian. It was dependent upon a cleansed life free of all unconfessed and unrenounced sin and upon a constant yielding of oneself to the Spirit's leadership. It was the practical working out of Paul's instruction to the Galatians: "If we live in the Spirit, let us also walk in the Spirit" (Gal. 5:25 KJV).

Another deepening experience for Bertha came in 1910 when she answered God's call on her life for mission service. A college student at the time, she struggled with the issue for several weeks, considering what sacrifices such a commitment would require. It would mean leaving home for many years, perhaps for life. Would her family approve? What settled it for her was the realization that Jesus Christ had given up the glories of Heaven, lived on the earth, and died a shameful death for her, all because it was the Father's will. How could she do any less than obey His will? When she yielded to God's call, a joy filled her heart that never left her.[7]

Prelude to Revival

When Bertha first arrived in China she became concerned very quickly about the low level of spirituality and commitment among Chinese believers. This was a burden shared by all the other missionaries as well.[8] They believed that a genuine revival was the only answer. Their conviction about this was strengthened as many of the missionaries experienced personal revivals in their own lives. God was moving in the Shantung province of China, preparing the land for a great outpouring of the Holy Spirit. He began by working in the hearts and lives of the missionaries.

During the summer months the missionaries had opportunities to attend annual conferences on various themes related to the spiritual life. These conferences were characterized by dynamic speakers and teachers and a powerful moving of the Holy Spirit to such a degree that many of the missionaries received deep refreshing and significant spiritual renewal. Bertha was one of these. The most significant change for her was learning the secret to consistent victory in her Christian life, to victory over her "old self." The key was in not trying to *overcome* the flesh—an impossible task—but in regarding it as *dead*: crucified with Christ. She realized that she had been wrongly struggling to crucify herself, rather than consider it already dead in Christ.[9] It was the truth that Paul taught the Romans when he wrote, "Likewise reckon ye also yourselves to be dead indeed unto sin, but alive unto God through Jesus Christ our Lord" (Rom. 6:11 KJV). Bertha explained the truth this way: "You cannot consecrate the old sinful self to God; you assign it to death."[10]

Bertha and the other missionaries felt an increasing burden from the Lord to pray for revival in China. This became so intense that they set aside the first day of each month for that specific purpose. They maintained this practice faithfully for several years before revival came. This committed, consistent discipline of prayer was one of the catalysts for the great revival that swept across the Shantung province, and indeed all of China, in 1927.

Another catalyst in the revival was an Evangelical Lutheran missionary from Norway named Marie Monsen. God used this deeply spiritual woman to spark revival fires wherever she went. In March 1927, she fled to the Chinese port city of Chefoo to escape political unrest further inland. Many other missionaries had taken temporary refuge in Chefoo also. Among them were Bertha and the other Southern Baptist missionaries whom she worked with. They invited Marie Monsen to share her testimony with them. Marie told of her experiences in Bible teaching and evangelism in the field, and also of the many instances she had seen of sick people being healed by the grace of God. The testimony of divine healing was a new and unusual concept for the Baptist missionaries, yet they were profoundly moved and touched by Marie Monsen's words.[11]

Marie believed that a great revival was coming to China and that it would come through the Baptists. When Dr. Charles L. Culpepper, one of the Baptist missionaries and the president of the small Baptist seminary in Shantung, asked her why it would be the Baptists, she answered, "Because you, more than any others, have fulfilled the promise of 2 Chronicles 7:14."[12]

The Shantung Revival

If any single event can be said to be the "beginning" of the Shantung revival, it was the powerful prayer meeting in March 1927, which involved Marie Monsen and the Baptist missionaries. The Holy Spirit inspired brokenness and deep confession of personal sin on the part of the missionaries. They resolved differences between one another and there was great cleansing of their lives and hearts. The primary purpose of the prayer meeting was to pray for the physical healing of Mrs. Ola Culpepper, Dr. Culpepper's wife, who had suffered for many years from optic neuritis—the decay of the optic nerve. It was a painful and degenerative condition. Although she was slowly going blind, Mrs. Culpepper could still see relatively well with glasses.

After the time of confession and cleansing, the missionaries laid hands on Mrs. Culpepper and prayed for her. The Spirit was so strong that when two Chinese cooks who worked at the mission and who had great animosity toward each other walked into the room, they were immediately brought under deep conviction. They confessed their sins to each other and accepted Christ as their Savior on the spot. After this Mrs. Culpepper testified that her pain was completely gone. It never returned. Although the vision in her most severely damaged eye was not completely restored, her vision in both eyes improved significantly and permanently.[13]

Although everyone in the group was rejoicing at the goodness and grace of God, Bertha suddenly felt convicted by their behavior. She told the others how inconsistent it seemed to spend so much time in confession, soul-searching, and prayer for each other when they had never done so in order to pray for the spiritual awakening of the Chinese people. Bertha's words hit the group like a thunderclap. As Bertha described it:

> Our mountaintop of ecstasy suddenly became a valley of humiliation. We all went to our knees in contrite confession for having been so careless as to have gone along supposing that we were right with the Lord, while holding all kinds of attitudes which could have kept the Lord's living water from flowing through us to the Chinese.[14]

From this beginning the revival began to spread as the missionaries returned to their various mission stations. It next affected the Chinese pastors and Bible-teaching women in the mission schools, and from them it spread into the general Chinese population. Confession of sin, restitution, and a strong emphasis on verifying one's genuine conversion to Christ by being "born of the

Spirit" were hallmarks of this tremendous awakening. The progress of the revival demonstrated the spiritual principle that "cleansing precedes fullness, and the in-filling of the Holy Spirit precedes joy and effective service."[15]

The Holy Spirit moved mightily until every church in the Shantung province had been affected. Many nominal church members who had never truly trusted Christ for salvation were genuinely converted. Many other believers in the churches experienced significant deepening in their relationships with Christ. There was a renewed burden for evangelism and a greatly increased hunger for God and for His Word. Thousands of believers experienced the joy of the Lord as never before and were filled with the Spirit, discovering for the first time the power of God for evangelism, discipleship, and service. As believers got their lives right with God and with each other, relationships were healed and true Christian fellowship became possible. People outside the churches saw the change that occurred in the lives of the revived believers. As a result, countless numbers of Chinese were brought to Christ.[16]

The Shantung revival made a significant impact on the Chinese churches throughout the land. The direct and immediate effects of the revival continued into the 1930's and beyond. In many ways, the effects are still being felt. Nothing that God does occurs without purpose. The awakening of the Christian Church in China came at just the right time to strengthen it and prepare it for the dark years ahead—years of danger and oppression first by the Japanese occupiers before and during World War II and then by the Communists. Without the awakening, the Christian Church in China probably would not have survived.

Days of Occupation

Bertha's experiences in China both before and during the Shantung revival set the tone and pattern for the rest of her life. Once she understood the principles of dying to self and how to be filled with the Spirit on a continuing basis, her life was never again the same. The secret was to keep her "sins confessed up to date." It was important to keep a short sin account before God—to confess and renounce sin as soon as the Holy Spirit revealed it to her. This is the same principle that she taught countless believers through the remaining years of her life.

When the Japanese invaded China in the spring of 1937, Bertha faced a dilemma. The primary missionary couple she worked with in Tsining were in the United States on furlough; she was the only missionary in the town. The American government had urged all Americans to leave the country and declared that it would not be responsible for the safety or welfare of any who decided to stay. Bertha debated what to do. Through prayer she became convinced that she should stay. It was God who had placed her in China, not the American government. She could not bear to leave the Chinese people, particularly the Chinese Christians who would be in such hardship.[17]

While war raged in the countryside in every direction from Tsining, Bertha labored faithfully and courageously. She opened the church for daily services, focusing on sharing the gospel to win people to Christ. She opened her home for any to come who wanted personal help in making decisions to receive Christ. Bertha knew that many of these Chinese would soon be fleeing from the Japanese; she knew that many of them would die. She was deeply concerned that they come to Christ and be firmly established in the faith while there was time. She regularly visited the local hospital to talk with the wounded soldiers and tell them about Jesus.[18]

Bertha made a practice of seeking God's specific, direct guidance for every move she made. There were so many needs that effective ministry was possible no other way. She could not address everyone, so she depended on God to show her where to go, what to do, and who to talk to. In this way she walked with God as He led her to where He was already working.

Bertha Smith: Walking in the Spirit

After Tsining fell to the Japanese, the mission compound where Bertha lived and worked housed many refugees, most of them women. Japanese soldiers were constantly looking for girls and young women and more than once Bertha squared off face to face with the soldiers, protecting those whom God had placed under her care. She had a holy boldness born from many years of intimate prayer and fellowship with Christ. Bertha was totally surrendered to God and trusted Him absolutely, and He protected, provided, and guided her steps. After the United States entered the war Bertha and other American missionaries were interned for a time in the mission compound. Bertha eventually was given an opportunity to return to the United States. This time she took it and did not return to China until after the war.

Bertha's Legacy

After the Communist takeover of China, all Christian missionaries were forced to leave the country. The Lord opened a door for Bertha, now 60, to become the first Southern Baptist missionary on the island of Formosa (Taiwan). There she labored faithfully for ten years, planting churches, teaching seminary classes, and helping to firmly establish the mission work on the island. In December 1958, she retired from active missionary service and returned to her hometown of Cowpens, South Carolina. God was not yet through with Bertha Smith, however.

For almost 30 years until her death in 1988 just five months short of her 100th birthday, Bertha Smith was in demand to speak at churches and conferences all over America. She felt that God had told her to "go home and tell" Christians in America about revival and being filled with the Spirit and to encourage them to seek and pray for spiritual awakening in America such as had occurred in China during the Shantung revival. During her travels and constant speaking engagements she touched thousands of lives. She was totally surrendered to Jesus Christ to the very end. A month before her death she led a Chinese businessman to Christ in Spartanburg, South Carolina.[19]

In addition to a legacy of changed lives in China, America, and other parts of the world, Bertha Smith left a legacy in the form of the Peniel Prayer Center, a retreat center for spiritual life conferences that was built near the home where she grew up in Cowpens. The Center continues today to provide opportunities for believers to learn the principles of revival, the Spirit-filled life, and spiritual victory that Bertha Smith so exemplified throughout her life.

The secret of Bertha Smith's courage and effectiveness throughout a century-long life is that she learned how to die to self: to regard herself as being dead to sin but alive to God through Jesus Christ (see Rom. 6:11). That is the key to spiritual victory, to personal revival, and to effectiveness in ministry. Bertha Smith lived her life with spiritual courage and holy boldness because, like the apostle Paul, she knew that "to live is Christ, and to die is gain" (Phil. 1:21).

Another woman on the front lines also experienced occupation by a foreign army—Corrie ten Boom. Her life and story of simple obedience to God in the face of imprisonment has inspired many thousands of people. Join with me as we glimpse into the life of this woman in her day of courage.

Endnotes

1. Lewis Drummond, *Miss Bertha: Woman of Revival* (Nashville, TN: Broadman and Holman Publishers, 1996), 100-102.
2. Bertha Smith, *Go Home and Tell* (Nashville, TN: Broadman & Holman, 1995), 90.
3. Drummond, *Miss Bertha*, 102.
4. Drummond, *Miss Bertha*, 5-6.
5. Bertha Smith, *How the Spirit Filled My Life* (Nashville, TN: Broadman Press, 1973), 22.
6. Drummond, *Miss Bertha*, 17.
7. Drummond, *Miss Bertha*, 24.
8. Drummond, *Miss Bertha*, 46.

9. Smith, *How the Spirit Filled My Life*, 29.
10. Drummond, *Miss Bertha*, 40.
11. Drummond, *Miss Bertha*, 48-49.
12. Drummond, *Miss Bertha*, 49.
13. C.L. Culpepper, *The Shantung Revival* (Dallas, TX: Crescendo Publications, 1971), 13-14.
14. Smith, *Go Home and Tell*, 40.
15. Drummond, *Miss Bertha*, 54.
16. Culpepper, *The Shantung Revival*, 72-73.
17. Smith, *Go Home and Tell*, 96-98.
18. Drummond, *Miss Bertha*, 121-123.
19. Drummond, *Miss Bertha*, 285.

Chapter 10

Corrie ten Boom: No Pit So Deep

As arrests of Jews in the streets became more frequent, I had begun picking up and delivering work for our Jewish customers myself so that they would not have to venture into the center of town. And so one evening in the early spring of 1942 I was in the home of a doctor and his wife....

The Heemstras and I were talking about the things that were discussed whenever a group of people got together in those days, rationing and the news from England, when down the stairs piped a childish voice.

"Daddy! You didn't tuck us in!"

Dr. Heemstra was on his feet in an instant. With an apology to his wife and me he hurried upstairs and in a minute we heard a game of hide-and-seek going and the shrill laughter of two children.

That was all. Nothing had changed. Mrs. Heemstra continued with her recipe for stretching the tea ration with rose leaves. And yet everything was changed. For in that instant, reality broke through the numbness that had grown in me since the invasion. At any minute there might be a rap on this door. These children, this mother and father, might be ordered to the back of a truck.

Dr. Heemstra came back to the living room and the conversation rambled on. But under the words a prayer was forming in my heart.

"Lord Jesus, I offer myself for Your people. In any way. Any place. Any time."

And then an extraordinary thing happened.

Even as I prayed, that waking dream passed again before my eyes. I saw again those four black horses and the Grote Markt. As I had on the night of the invasion I scanned the passengers drawn so unwillingly behind them. Father, Betsie, Willem, myself—leaving Haarlem, leaving all that was sure and safe—going where?[1]

This is how Corrie ten Boom, a 50-year-old unmarried Dutch watchmaker, described the turning point in her life. Shortly after this Corrie and other members of her family put their lives on the line to harbor and assist frightened people who had become enemies of the state for no other reason than that they were Jews. In defiance of the repressive Nazi government that occupied their beloved Holland, the ten Booms hid fugitive Jews in their home and helped them escape to freedom. By the time it was all over, Corrie's father, her oldest sister, and a nephew had died in concentration camps. Other family members spent time in jail and Corrie herself survived ten months of imprisonment, first in a Dutch prison, then in a concentration camp in Holland, and finally in the infamous Ravensbruck camp in Germany, where 96,000 women died.

A Pattern of Preparation

From all external appearances there was very little about Corrie ten Boom during the first 50 years of her life that would lead anyone to expect that she would ever become involved in such dangerous activities. She lived all those years in the same house where she was born: an ancient structure known as the Beje that housed her father's watch and clock shop on the first floor and the family's living quarters on the floors above. Like her oldest sister Betsie, Corrie helped her father in the watch shop. She took such an interest in the work that she eventually became the first licensed woman watchmaker in Holland. Corrie and her family were regular, active members of the Dutch Reformed Church. These early years were characterized by a regular, comfortable routine to everyday life.

Yet within this familiar sameness of day-to-day life God was preparing Corrie and her family for the great acts of courage and devotion that they would be called upon to perform during the years of Nazi oppression. Corrie was only five years old when she accepted Jesus Christ as her Savior and Lord. When the great crisis came in her life, she had already spent 45 years walking with Him. For more than 20 of those years Corrie planned and led weekly worship services especially for feeble-minded and retarded people in the city. The daily routine of life in the Beje included family Bible reading and prayer at breakfast in the morning and before retiring for the night. Despite the family's modest means, the ten Booms opened their home to people in need. Consequently, the presence of guests and strangers around the ten Boom dining table was a familiar sight to Corrie.

The ten Booms believed that the Christian faith was to be lived out, not just believed and talked about. Day by day their lives were focused on relating to people through the ordinary circumstances of life, just as Jesus did. Such Christ-like living became almost as natural to them as breathing. When the Nazi occupation of Holland forced extraordinary circumstances upon them and brought scores of desperate people their way, the ten Booms responded according to the pattern established over a lifetime of faithfulness to God. Corrie came to understand later how God prepares us for what lies ahead. She said, "I know that the experiences of our lives, when we let God use them, become the mysterious and perfect preparation for the work He will give us to do."[2]

Working for the Underground

After the Germans occupied Holland in the spring of 1940, conditions of life for the Dutch people gradually deteriorated and grew more and more repressive. Every person was required to carry identification at all times, which had to be presented at the demand of any member of the occupying forces. Food and other goods were severely rationed. Young men between the ages of 16 and 30 were subject at any time to be hauled off to work as virtual slave laborers in German factories. Even minor offenses could mean imprisonment without trial for indefinite periods.

The most oppressive of all was the increasing persecution of Jews. All Jews were required to wear a Star of David made of bright yellow cloth that was prominently displayed on their outer clothing. Verbal abuse and ridicule on the streets led to the routine vandalism of Jewish businesses. Before long, Jews were being rounded up without warning on the streets. Jewish homes were raided in the middle of the night and families carried away in the darkness.

The ten Booms became directly involved for the first time in November 1941, when Mr. Weil, the Jewish furrier across the street, was ejected from his shop by four German soldiers who smashed his display cases, carried off his furs, and threw his clothing and personal belongings into the street. During all this activity, Corrie and her sister Betsie quickly ushered the man to shelter in the Beje. That same evening, with the assistance of their brother Willem and his son Kik, Mr. Weil was taken to safety.[3]

By the summer of 1942 the Beje had become the center of an underground operation that focused on harboring Jews who were hiding from the Nazis and helping them escape to safety. All of the ten Booms were involved: Corrie, Betsie, and their father, all of whom lived in the Beje, as well as Corrie's brother Willem and his family and her older sister Nollie and her family, who lived in homes of their own. Corrie was regarded as the "leader" of the operation in the Beje.

It began on a small scale, harboring two or three fugitives for a day or two until arrangements could be made to lead them to safety. Within a very short time the operation grew to a more sophisticated level: an illegal radio carefully hidden beneath the stairs; stolen ration cards to provide escapees a means of getting food; an electrical buzzer system to warn of approaching trouble; a visual warning system to let outsiders know whether or not the coast was clear; their personal telephone secretly reconnected even though it was illegal for private families to have phones.

Eventually, the Beje became the permanent home for seven Jews who could not be placed elsewhere. They took their meals regularly at the ten Booms' table. A false wall was constructed in Corrie's bedroom on the top floor of the house, concealing behind it a crawl space 18 inches wide yet large enough for all seven "houseguests" to hide, for several days if necessary. Practice drills were held until all seven could be concealed without a trace in just over one minute. Such care was crucial to their survival in the event of a raid.

One of the things that sustained the ten Booms' underground operation was their sensitivity to God's leadership. Corrie learned to trust the direct leadership of God for specific decisions, particularly with regard to people. In a social and political environment in which the wisest human course was to trust no one, it nevertheless was necessary on occasion for Corrie to seek help from someone who could supply a particular need. The risk was in not knowing whether the person approached would be sympathetic or would betray the operation to the Nazi authorities. Time after time Corrie received what she called the "gift of knowledge"[4] when these decisions were needed. Her brother Willem had told Corrie to develop her own sources. When reflecting on this, Corrie realized another value of having lived quietly in the same place for years: They knew someone in every business and service in the city![5] As Corrie remembered:

> We didn't know, of course, the political views of all these people. But—and here I felt a strange leaping of my heart—God did! My job was simply to follow His leading one step at a time, holding every decision up to Him in prayer. I knew I was not clever or subtle or sophisticated; if the Beje was becoming a meeting place for need and supply, it was through some strategy far higher than mine.[6]

On February 28, 1944, after about 18 months of underground activity, the inevitable happened: the Beje was raided. The ten Booms were betrayed by a Dutch man working for the Nazis who had posed as a Jew needing help. During the raid Corrie, Betsie, and their father were arrested, along with numerous others who appeared at the Beje unaware that anything was wrong. The seven Jews sheltered there were not discovered, however; all had made it into the secret room in Corrie's bedroom. After several days in hiding, they were able to escape to safety.

The ten Booms and the other prisoners were taken to the local police station for processing, where they spent the night under guard in a gymnasium. The next day they were taken to the town square and put on a bus for prison. In all, several dozen people in the underground were taken, including Corrie's brother Willem and sister Nollie. The scene at the square seemed strangely familiar to Corrie. Then she realized that she had seen it twice before in a vision: once on the night Germany invaded Holland and once on the night of her "turning point," during her visit to the Heemstras.[7]

Neither Corrie nor any of the others knew what was in store as they were driven away from their homes by their captors. They knew only that their lives were in God's hands. In reality, the next phase of God's plan for them—the plan for which He had been preparing them all through the years—was about to unfold.

Corrie ten Boom: No Pit So Deep

If I Make My Bed in Hell...

Ten years after the family's arrest, a Dutch policeman still remembered the ten Booms' first night when they were held in the police station gymnasium. He told Corrie:

> I shall never forget that night. There was an atmosphere as if there were a feast, even though most of you were on your way to die in prison. I remember that just before your father tried to sleep, he said, "Children, let us pray together." Tired from the ordeal, but with a radiance on his face, he offered comfort from God's Word, Psalms 91:1 [KJV]: *He that dwelleth in the secret place of the most High shall abide under the shadow of the Almighty.*[8]

It was the family's faith and confidence in God's protection that would sustain them through the horrors that lay ahead.

The next day the prisoners were transported to a Dutch prison in the coastal town of Scheveningen. There Corrie and Betsie were held for several months. While in prison they received word that Willem, Nollie, and all the others taken in the raid at the Beje had been released after a few weeks. They learned eventually that their father, well into his 80's, had died after only ten days in prison.

In the late spring of 1944 Betsie and Corrie were transferred to Vught, a concentration camp on Dutch soil. There, using a small Bible they had received from Nollie while they were in prison, Corrie and Betsie held secret prayer meetings in the barracks at night, sharing the light and hope of Jesus Christ with the other women. It was during this time also that Corrie found in Christ the power to forgive the man who had betrayed them to the Gestapo. In fact, the final letter Corrie wrote from prison before being sent to Ravensbruck was to this man. Her letter declared her forgiveness and pointed him to Jesus Christ as the source of eternal salvation.[9]

As the Allied forces advanced after the invasion of Europe in June 1944, the camp at Vught was evacuated and Corrie and Betsie were transported to Ravensbruck, a larger and much more brutal camp in Germany. If any place could have earned the designation of "hell on earth," it would have been Ravensbruck. Yet it was here, in the midst of the darkness of human sin and brutality, that the light of Christ shone brightly in the lives and witness of the ten Boom sisters.

God encouraged them by confirming His continuing presence with them through several miraculous events. First, He made it possible for them to smuggle their Bible, a bottle of vitamins, and a sweater past the careful eyes and searching hands of the guards.[10] Betsie's health, never very good, was deteriorating and she needed the sweater for warmth and the vitamins for strength. The Bible they needed for their own faith and as a means to share the love of God in a place where love had died.

Second, the tiny bottle of liquid vitamins served not only Betsie's needs, but also the needs of other sick women in the barracks. Day after day, week after week, dose after dose, the vitamins kept coming long after the contents should have been exhausted. It was a miracle that paralleled the biblical story of the poor widow of Zarephath, who gave the prophet Elijah a room in her home. She gave Elijah food when she had none to spare for herself and her son. By the providence of God her small supply of meal and oil did not run out until the drought ended in Israel (see 1 Kings 17:9-16). In Ravensbruck, the very day a prisoner who worked in the camp hospital smuggled a supply of vitamins to the ten Booms' barracks, not another drop appeared from their bottle.[11]

Third, the barracks were heavily infested with fleas. Corrie could not understand why Betsie insisted on thanking God for the fleas, but they did anyway in accordance with Paul's admonition, "In every thing give thanks: for this is the will of God in Christ Jesus concerning you" (1 Thess. 5:18 KJV).[12] They soon discovered that the camp guards rarely came into the barracks because of the fleas. Corrie and Betsie were free almost without hindrance to pray, witness, and read the Bible to the ever-increasing circle of women who gathered to hear the words of hope and life.[13]

Corrie ten Boom: No Pit So Deep

As Corrie and Betsie walked with God in Ravensbruck, He used them to bless hundreds of other prisoners. He also spoke to them, especially Betsie, regarding the future. They had a vision of a beautiful home in spacious surroundings; a home where concentration camp survivors could come for spiritual, emotional, and psychological healing; a home where they could live until they were ready to return to the normal world.[14] Another vision was of a German concentration camp, transformed after the war into a home where people warped by the philosophy of hate, force, and violence taught by the Nazis, could learn of love, peace, and the forgiveness of Christ.[15]

Betsie's health continued to decline until she was released from outside work and eventually was put in the camp hospital. It was December 1944. While in the hospital, Betsie shared with Corrie a final dream:

> We must tell people what we have learned here. We must tell them that there is no pit so deep that He is not deeper still. They will listen to us, Corrie, because we have been here....By the first of the year, Corrie, we will be out of prison![16]

Betsie's words came true. The very next day she died in the hospital. When Corrie came to see Betsie, she witnessed another miracle. The day before, Betsie's face had been hollow from hunger and disease and deeply lined from care and grief. Now, in death, her face was full and young again. All signs of disease and pain were gone. As Corrie described her: "In front of me was the Betsie of Haarlem, happy and at peace. Stronger! Freer! This was the Betsie of heaven, bursting with joy and health."[17]

Three days later, Corrie received her notice of discharge. Her release was delayed for several days while she was treated for swelling in her legs. Finally, on January 1, 1945, she walked out of Ravensbruck a free woman. Now it was time to tell the world what she and Betsie had learned.

Corrie's Legacy

As soon as she was free and returned home, Corrie began to speak wherever she had opportunity. God immediately opened the door for the home for concentration camp survivors to become a reality. A wealthy Dutch widow donated her elegant suburban estate and the home received its first residents in June 1945. It remains in operation today under the auspices of the Dutch Reformed Church.[18]

In 1946 Betsie's second vision, the home for rehabilitation and renewal for Germans, was fulfilled with the reopening of Darmstadt, a former concentration camp in Germany. Under the direction of the German Lutheran Church, it remained in operation until 1960.[19]

Corrie embarked on another journey of nearly 40 years, traveling the world as a self-described "tramp for the Lord," visiting 61 countries on both sides of the Iron Curtain. Wherever she went, to whomever she spoke, she shared the truth that she and Betsie had learned in Ravensbruck: that Jesus can turn loss into glory.[20] During the remainder of her life she influenced countless thousands, perhaps even millions, by the testimony of her life and her witness to God's faithfulness. As a "tramp for the Lord" Corrie sought God's direct guidance concerning where to go and how long to stay, trusting Him to provide for her every need. She never appealed for money or other kinds of financial support. This was part of her absolute trust in the God who had sustained her so absolutely throughout her life and particularly in Ravensbruck.

Corrie ten Boom's courage came from a source beyond herself. It lay in the One for whom she had lived exclusively since the age of five; the One whom she had met daily in the pages of the Bible; the One to whom she prayed regularly. In all her years she never found Him to fail. Corrie ten Boom found courage because she knew that God is good and that God is faithful. He never puts on us more than we can bear. Whatever He requires of us He equips us to do. Corrie walked with God and in His strength bore the unbearable and prevailed to victory.

Let's ask for the grace to walk the crucified life that this woman on the front lines lived for the glory of her Master.

Now let us turn the pages of *Women on the Front Lines* to one of this generation's women of courage—Jackie Pullinger-To. My husband calls Jackie a modern-day apostolic evangelist walking in the path where Aimee Semple McPherson and others have trodden. All I know is, when she speaks, the truth of the cross comes across more clearly than through any other minister of our day! So let's have this revolutionary figure take the stand as we get a glimpse of the shadow of bold faith she is casting.

Endnotes

1. Corrie ten Boom, *The Hiding Place*, in *Corrie ten Boom: Her Story* (New York: Inspirational Press, a division of BBS Publishing Corporation, by arrangement with Chosen Books, Inc., and Fleming H. Revell, a division of Baker Book House Company, 1995), 57-58.
2. ten Boom, *The Hiding Place*, 17.
3. David Wallington, "The Secret Room: The Story of Corrie ten Boom," Soon Online Magazine (London: Soon Educational Publications), August 1998. <http://www.soon.org.uk/true_stories/holocaust.htm>, 3.
4. ten Boom, *The Hiding Place*, 73.
5. ten Boom, *The Hiding Place*, 65.
6. ten Boom, *The Hiding Place*, 65.
7. ten Boom, *The Hiding Place*, 102.
8. Joan Winmill Brown, *Corrie: The Lives She's Touched* (Old Tappan, NJ: Fleming H. Revell Company, 1979), 49.
9. Bill Johnson, "Corrie ten Boom: How to Live for Christ When Evil Is in Power," 1997. <http://www.fbclubbock.org/library/lesson/corrie.htm>.

10. ten Boom, *The Hiding Place*, 141-142.
11. ten Boom, *The Hiding Place*, 148-149.
12. ten Boom, *The Hiding Place*, 145-146.
13. ten Boom, *The Hiding Place*, 153.
14. Brown, *Corrie: The Lives*, 63
15. Carole C. Carlson, *Corrie ten Boom: Her Life, Her Faith* (Old Tappan, NJ: Fleming H. Revell Company, 1983), 117.
16. ten Boom, *The Hiding Place*, 159.
17. ten Boom, *The Hiding Place*, 160.
18. Elizabeth Sherrill, "Since Then," Guideposts Magazine, 1983, in ten Boom, *The Hiding Place*, 176.
19. Sherrill, "Since Then," 176.
20. Sherrill, "Since Then," 176-177.

Chapter 11

Jackie Pullinger-To: Lighting the Darkness

I loved the dark city. I loved wandering down the narrow lanes which were like some exaggerated stageset. It upset me to see twelve- or thirteen-year-old prostitutes and to learn that these girls were not free, having been sold by parents or boyfriends. It troubled me to meet their minders—the aged mamasans who sat on the orange boxes in the streets luring the Walled City voyeurs with promises of "she's very good, very young, very cheap". I noticed their hands, which were scarred on the back with needle marks from the heroin injections which made the job bearable. Or maybe the job was to pay for the heroin.

There were bodies at that time lying in the streets near the drug dens: they could have been alive or dead after "chasing the dragon" (a popular way of inhaling heroin through a tube held over heated tinfoil). There were the "weather men" who guarded the alley exits and the entrances to the heroin huts where up to a hundred people "chased" in lonely chorus. I saw thousands of poor people living in one-room dwellings: many were so crammed that they had to sleep in shifts because they could not all lie down at the same time. I saw some who still lived with pigs, neither able to see the light of day....

I loved this dark place. I hated what was happening in it but I wanted to be nowhere else. I dreamed of walking into heroin dens, laying hands on men and seeing them set free. I dreamed of praying with the blind in the dark lanes, touching them, and watching their eyes open. It was almost as if I could already see another city in its place and that city was ablaze with light. It was my dream. There were no more crying, no more death or pain. The sick were healed, addicts set free, the hungry filled. There were families for orphans, homes for the homeless, and new dignity for those who had lived in shame. I had no idea how to bring this about but with "visionary zeal" imagined introducing the Walled City people to the one who could change it all: Jesus.[1]

Jackie Pullinger-To had talked about being a missionary since she was five years old, even though for many years she had no real idea what a missionary was. She had a conventional English upbringing—attending a boarding school and being confirmed in the Church of England. Higher education followed at the Royal College of Music, where Jackie studied piano and oboe.[2] Upon completing her degree she began a career teaching music. However, she could not escape the feeling that she needed to give her life to something.

Although she had been confirmed in the Church of England, the Christian faith did not become real to Jackie until she was in college. She encountered a group of friends who obviously enjoyed their relationship with Jesus and could discuss their experience and feelings about it with ease and joy. This concept intrigued Jackie. She states, "This was the first time that I had met Christians who did not look unhappy, guilty or grim, and my music college Christian Union...had only served to confirm my worst fears and impressions of earnest organists trying to get to heaven. I preferred brass players. I avoided the Christians while unable to avoid the unhappy conviction that at some time God himself would nail me for my shortcomings and I would have to account for my life."[3]

From Music Teacher to Missionary

Through her new Christian friends, Jackie became confronted with the reality of Jesus Christ, His sacrifice on the cross, and the good news of God's love and forgiveness that was available through Jesus. It changed her life dramatically. After accepting Jesus as her Lord and Savior, she found herself filled with a great joy, and rather than becoming more limited and grim, her life became more fun than ever before. Sharing this good news with others became a spontaneous outpouring of her newfound joy and peace. She developed a great burden for those who did not know this joy and personal relationship with Jesus and who were lost and bound for hell.

God reawakened within Jackie her childhood dream of becoming a missionary, but she was a single woman and too young and unqualified to be accepted by any of the conventional missionary societies. Every door seemed shut, and she wondered if she had heard God correctly. Desperate for answers and direction, Jackie attended a special prayer meeting with friends, and there God spoke to her. He said, "Go. Trust Me, and I will lead you. I will instruct you and lead you in the way in which you shall go; I will guide you with My eye."

At that, Jackie knew that she must take action and obey. After much prayer and godly counsel, Jackie decided that God had doors to open for her that she had not yet seen. She decided to allow God to lead her directly and go on a daring adventure. She bought the cheapest boat ticket that she could find that stopped at the greatest number of countries and prayed for God's direction to know where to get off and how He wanted her to proceed from there.

So with this great act of faith, Jackie found herself stepping off a boat in Hong Kong in 1966 after traveling halfway around the globe. She had no missionary agency or organized support for her back in Britain, no job, and no contacts. She had very little money and no clear direction of what God had in store for her, but she had the assurance that God had called her and would continue to direct her.

The Walled City

Soon after her arrival in Hong Kong, Jackie was hired to teach music three afternoons a week in a primary school operated by a Mrs. Donnithorne. The school was located within a six-acre enclave of Hong Kong known as the Walled City. One of its Chinese names is "Hak Nam," which means "darkness." Cramped, secluded, and filthy, the Walled City was home to anywhere from 30,000 to 60,000 people—no one knew for sure how many—and was a haven of opium dens, heroin huts, brothels, pornography theaters, illegal gambling, smuggling, and all other kinds of vice. Virtually ignored by the rest of Hong Kong, the Walled City was accessible only through dark, narrow alleys between shops located on its outer edges. There were no sanitary facilities—refuse and excrement were simply dumped out in the streets and alleys—and electricity was illegally tapped from supplies outside the City.[4]

Daily life in the Walled City was regulated and defined by various Triad gangs who controlled the region's activities of vice, extortion, and crime. The boundaries of each gang's territory were clearly defined, and violence between rival gangs was frequent. Gang membership provided a sense of family and acceptance for young Chinese men that they rarely found elsewhere in "Hak Nam." The city called "darkness" was in great need of the light of Jesus, and Jackie was becoming a torchbearer for her generation.

Jackie's teaching work gave her access to the Walled City, and she began trying to relate to the people she met there. She sought to share Christ as she had opportunity. Externally, the Walled City was one of the most revolting places on earth, yet every time she entered it, Jackie felt a profound sense of joy. This confirmed for her that she was where God had called her.[5]

At first Jackie met with little success. She had zeal but few obvious results. This was made apparent one day as she tried to share Jesus with a corner prostitute:

> She was an old-young prostitute who squatted all day long over a sewer with little custom and no looks. She had no radio, she could not read. She looked dead before her life had even started. I tried the "Jesus loves you" routine on her and touched her to show her I meant it. She looked terrified.
>
> "You've made a mistake. You don't know who I am. You're not supposed to touch people like me."
>
> Looking back now I can see how ridiculous it was to be walking down alleyways talking intensely of Jesus. Of course, no one could respond to words about Christ. They had never met him and had no evidence of his love. When I checked, I found he had never done it that way either; instead of declaring "I love you", Jesus had shown his love through action. He opened the eyes of the blind man, caused the lame to leap for joy and fed five thousand hungry people full to bursting.[6]

She Showed Them Jesus

This thought planted a dream deep within this radical disciple. She wanted these desperately needy people to know Jesus, but in order for them to meet Him, she realized that she must first show Him to them. Jackie began a youth club to reach out to the young people of the Walled City. This club enabled her to befriend young people who were members of the feared Triad organizations. God touched her in a new way and she began to pray intensely for the people within the dark Walled City. Suddenly light began to break through the darkness around her and lives began to be changed one by one.

Jackie took seriously her call to help the people at their point of need. She went to bat for the poor and helped them obtain assistance and housing from government agencies. She planned activities to give the young people alternatives to the vices around them. She looked for ways to help and minister to the most "poor in spirit and body" of those around her, which ultimately led her to preaching Jesus and ministering to the needs of the drug addicts. Jackie discovered that a sincere heart, prayer, and praise could often help an addict go through withdrawal in a short and relatively painless way.[7]

It was not long after this that Jackie found herself sitting across a tea table from one of the most powerful Triad bosses in the Walled City. He had become frustrated with the problem of addiction among his own followers. Although the Triads regularly dealt in drug trafficking, actual addiction often made their members useless to their gang. He amazingly proposed to give Jackie the addicts of his group to get them off drugs, but not budging, Jackie refused to help the young men break free of their heroin addiction only to return to their lives of violence and crime. The leader then made her an offer never heard before; he told her that he would release from the Triad any of its members who wanted to follow Jesus. (Triad membership was always considered a lifetime commitment, and persons attempting to leave Triad membership often would be severely punished.) What an offer! What an opportunity for her Lord!

St. Stephen's Society

This arrangement gave Jackie an even greater "green light" for ministry to the drug addicts of the Walled City. She found that many of the people she helped among the addicted, poor, crippled, and homeless literally had nowhere to go and no way to start a new life. Eventually this led to the development of special homes for them and to the beginning of the St. Stephen's Society, which became actively involved in all aspects of help and rehabilitation to the people of Hong Kong who were in need of its services.

Jackie's one-woman crusade within the Walled City not only led to the development of a very successful drug rehabilitation program but also gave birth to an active, vibrant, Spirit-empowered Church within the confines of the Walled City. Special group homes and ministries were developed, and ultimately, the government gave them facilities in which to continue their work and house the needy on a greater scale. These facilities became known as Hang Fook Camp, and they served as base of operations for Jackie and the St. Stephen's Society for several years. But her emphasis was the preaching of the cross, holy abandonment, and the power of prayer.

The Power of Prayer

My husband Jim and I have had the privilege of hearing this stunning evangelist tell of her modern-day exploits with God. Her keys are the cross of Christ and a revelation of our dependency on God through prayer. This power of prayer is no better demonstrated than in her story of Alie.

> ...Alie...was studying to be a Buddhist monk. Alie was also facing court charges as an alleged accomplice with seven other men in the murder of a rival drug lord.

> Jackie began to visit this particular Hong Kong jail every week to minister and to testify to these men, and specifically to Alie. Four of the men came to the Lord almost immediately. But though Jackie visited the jail every day for nine months testifying to Alie about Jesus through a thick glass partition, he was unmoved.

> Alie wouldn't admit it, but he was very afraid of dying for a crime that he did not do. Week after week, Jackie...continued to minister to him. "I know that you are afraid, Alie. I know that you are terrified of death, but I want to tell you that there is a loving God. There is a God of justice who knows all things and He is a Father

of mercy. And I have enlisted Christians from all across the world to pray and fast on every Wednesday for you, Alie." Although Alie heard and understood the things Jackie was saying, he still refused to come to the Lord because his heart was hard.

One day the governor of the jail and a jail attendant passed by Alie's cell and remarked to one another that they smelled something. They did not know what the strange fragrance was, but they thought it was some kind of delicate perfume with a fragrant odor. They began asking Alie questions about the fragrance, but Alie said, "What smell?" Perplexed, the two men asked other inmates about the smell, as the entire jail cell took on the fragrant odor of this strange perfume.

Finally, the governor of the jail sent authorities into Alie's cell. They searched his body and found nothing. When they sniffed the air around him, they nodded and said, "Yes, the smell is here." Yet Alie still smelled nothing. When the guards left, Alie began to ask himself, *What is that smell?* Then a little word trickled down inside him. It was this simple message: "Oh, it is Wednesday!" Suddenly, he remembered Jackie's words. *He was smelling prayer!* He realized his entire jail cell was filled with the fragrant aroma of the prayers of the saints.[8]

As a result, Alie eventually accepted Jesus as his Savior. Such stories are common in Jackie's ministry, due to the prayers of faithful saints.

Transitions With Hong Kong and With Jackie

The Walled City itself was torn down in 1992, and The Kowloon Walled City Park was opened in 1995. In 1996, Jackie and her organization were requested to leave Hang Fook Camp. Because no alternative accommodations became available, the St. Stephen's Society had to disperse and decentralize its activities. At last report, this seeming "dispersion" has actually sparked greater life and activity among the people and churches of Hong Kong, and many individuals have risen up to continue the society's ministry on a one-to-one and house-to-house basis. It has become a wonderful expression of the Body of Christ in action. As Jackie has stated, "All of this is what I've been sharing and teaching on for years and with the loss of a big centre it's meant that people have taken more responsibility for their own groups and lives....we are [also] continuing on a regular basis to do outreaches, feeding the poor, the old people, street sleepers, etc..."[9]

In 1997, Hong Kong was turned over to the Chinese government. Yet lives continue to be changed as a result of the work Jackie began in the late 1960's. The St. Stephen's Society also has broadened its vision to include missions and ministry throughout Asia. Jackie also travels periodically to Britain and the United States to speak and to teach. She actively exhorts believers that "every Christian must be directly involved with reaching out to the poor—meaning: people with needs which they are unable to help themselves, such as addictions, abject poverty, victims of child abuse or spouse abuse,"[10] and as a result, even more lives continue to be transformed.

Eventually, after years of serving her Lord as a single, white, "proper" British woman in an Asian, crime-ridden society, Jackie's life took another radical shift. She married a tall Chinese convert to the faith and thus became Jackie Pullinger-To.

Jackie's Legacy

Through Jackie's ministry in the Walled City over the years, hundreds of Chinese have come to Christ: drug dealers, drug addicts, prostitutes, gang members, and gang bosses. God was able to do a mighty work among the lost and outcast people of the Walled City in Hong Kong because a young English woman had the faith to believe that He would lead her and the courage to act on that faith. Jackie Pullinger-To entered Hong Kong with no human resources to fall back on. She had followed the Spirit's leading to Hong Kong and knew that she was totally dependent upon God for her protection, resources, and success. Her life is a testimony to the truth that there is no limit to what one person can accomplish when he or she commits him or herself completely into the hands of the Lord.

Taking the Baton

These valiant women warriors, these healers, brave souls, and pioneers whose lives we have just looked at, are only a few of the many whom God has used through the years. Regardless of their differences in calling and life work, passion for Jesus and compassion for people is the banner they all have carried. But simply reading about them is not enough! I hope that these chapters don't just inspire you; I hope they unsettle you. Yes, it's time for you and me to "seize the day"!

Endnotes

1. Jackie Pullinger, *Crack in the Wall* (London: Hodder & Stoughton, 1997), 7-8.
2. Jackie Pullinger, *Chasing the Dragon* (Ann Arbor, MI: Servant Books, 1982), 137.
3. Pullinger, *Crack in the Wall*, 8.
4. Pullinger, *Chasing the Dragon*, 34-36.
5. Pullinger, *Chasing the Dragon*, 39.
6. Pullinger, *Crack in the Wall*, 18-19.
7. Pullinger, *Crack in the Wall*, 26-32.
8. Jim Goll, *The Lost Art of Intercession* (Shippensburg, PA: Revival Press, 1997), 36-37.
9. Jackie Pullinger, "Where Are We Now," Worldscope Communigram. January 1997 <http://www.churchlink.com.au/churchlink/worldscope/communigram.jackie.html>.
10. "Report on the Meetings With Jackie Pullinger-To," Christians for Revival. 1998 <http://www.antioch.com.sg/th/cfr/jackie.html>.

Part III

Seize the Day!

Chapter 12

You Are Chosen!

Consider for a moment the nine women whose lives we have profiled in this book. They are so different from each other in race, nationality, culture, background, and time in history. What is the common bond between them? What connects Joan of Arc, Perpetua, Sojourner Truth, Harriet Tubman, Aimee Semple McPherson, Lydia Prince, Bertha Smith, Corrie ten Boom, and Jackie Pullinger-To? Very simply, they were *ordinary women* who knew an *extraordinary God*. When they gave to Him their very ordinariness, when they came to Him in their human weakness, He showed Himself strong on their behalf and used them in extraordinary ways.

You may feel that you are the least qualified for God to use and the most unlikely candidate for His Spirit to fall upon. Guess what? You're just the kind of person He chooses! God makes a point of choosing the weak things of the world to shame the mighty and the foolish things of the world to shame the wise (see 1 Cor. 1:27). God is revealed and glorified in your weakness. The apostle Paul himself knew this. He wrote to the Corinthians:

But He said to me, My grace (My favor and loving-kindness and mercy) is enough for you [sufficient against any danger and enables you to bear the trouble manfully]; for My strength and power are made perfect (fulfilled and completed) and show themselves most effective in [your] weakness. Therefore, I will all the more gladly glory in my weaknesses and infirmities, that the strength and power of Christ (the Messiah) may rest (yes, may pitch a tent over and dwell) upon me! (2 Corinthians 12:9)

Do you fall into the category of the weak, the ordinary, the least likely? If you do, take heart! You are a prime target for the Lord to come and wrap Himself around you. Isn't that great news?

Chosen Ones

Years ago I had a dream in which I was entering a large coliseum. It was in a foreign country and the king's court was about to convene. Every woman who entered the building was given a number. Mine was number 29. The king had not yet come out as I sat down to watch the proceedings. I ended up sitting next to a woman who simply despised me, no matter how hard I tried to be nice. For some reason I just irritated the daylights out of her. Anything nice I tried to do or say was like rubbing salt into a wound. She became extremely hostile to me and was constantly reviling me—putting cigarette ashes on my head and that kind of thing.

In this dream, during the preliminary proceedings prior to the king's appearance, someone was calling out the different numbers assigned to the women in the room. Whoever's number was called had to go spend the night with a man, whether or not she wanted to. The hateful woman next to me called out my number. I was so sickened at the thought of what I was supposed to do that I simply got up and ran out of the auditorium as fast as I could.

Unknown to me at the time, the king's son had come out and was going to choose his bride that day. He had heard my number, number 29, called and had seen me run away. He put his fingers to his lips and said, "I like that. She ran away from evil. I choose *her*!" Everyone began looking around, saying, "Where is she? Where did she go?"

Suddenly, I came back in dressed in regal robes. My face looked totally different. I knew it was me, but I didn't recognize myself. I approached the court and stood in front of the king's son. He kissed me and gave me a scepter. There were two thrones and we both turned around and sat down in them. That's how the dream ended.

I have come to understand since then that this dream wasn't just for me, but for all of us—the Bride of Christ. It is a dream of where the Lord wants to take us. We are His chosen ones, set apart before we were ever born. Paul told the Ephesians:

> *Even as [in His love] He chose us [actually picked us out for Himself as His own] in Christ before the foundation of the world, that we should be holy (consecrated and set apart for Him) and blameless in His sight, even above reproach, before Him in love* (Ephesians 1:4).

For years I asked the Lord, "God, what's the deal about number 29? What does it mean?" He answered my question by showing me Scriptures such as, "For I know the thoughts and plans that I have for you, says the Lord, thoughts and plans for welfare and peace and not for evil, to give you hope in your final outcome" (Jer. **29**:11); "But you are a chosen race, a royal priesthood, a dedicated nation, [God's] own purchased, special people, that you may set forth the wonderful deeds and display the virtues and perfections of Him Who called you out of darkness into His marvellous light" (1 Pet. **2:9**); Esther **2:9**, where Esther is given the choice place in the king's harem; and Psalm **29**, which talks about the voice of the Lord thundering, causing the deer to calf, stripping bare the forests, echoing across the waters, and *breaking open the way*. Then there is Acts **29**. Now, I know there is no chapter 29 to the Book of Acts. *We're writing it.* That's what we're called to come into. We have been chosen. That's what the number 29 means—chosen.

Being a Chosen One Has Responsibilities

When you accept yourself as among those whom God has chosen, you must understand that your position carries great responsibilities as well as privileges. I am really thankful that the Lord is bringing a release for women in ministry today. He is setting us free and unshackling our voices, our arms, our legs, and our hearts. In the midst of it all, though, we must be careful to keep our focus pure. In the days ahead we will have opportunities for far more battles than we can possibly endure. Therefore, we must choose wisely and carefully discern the battles that the Lord has given us to fight.

You see, the issue isn't the Lord's releasing women. The issue is the Lordship of Jesus Christ. We're not here to promote our own camp. Constant harping on "equality for women" comes from the wrong spirit. We want to build the Body of Christ, and that means focusing on *unity*. It means repairing the breach between men and women. We have to be very careful when we as women stand before anyone that we are not guilty of self-exaltation. Jesus told us in Luke 14:10 to take the lowest seat and to let the host invite us to a higher place. We should not presume to that higher place ourselves.

I know that in many cases women have assumed leadership or responsibility because men have failed to do so. Women have seen the need and jumped in. Unfortunately, many times they have done so out of a wrong spirit and have taken an inheritance that was not meant for them. God doesn't intend for it to be an "either-or" setup but a "both-and" arrangement. We are to be laborers *together* with God, as Paul says in First Corinthians 3:9. Whether we are men or women, we are to take our stations on the wall and do our jobs, thankfully receiving the inheritance that God has given us and running with it, all the while helping those next to us to do the same.

It's called servant leadership, and it requires a humble heart. You must be willing to take the low place and let God be the one who raises you up. If you want to be able to walk in the authority God wants to release to you, then you must learn how to walk *under* the authority that is over you—the Lord's authority. If you want to see release in your own life, then you must be in right relationship with the Lord and with those whom He has placed in authority over you. When you are in your proper place, doing God's will and exercising the gifts and function that He has given you in the Body of Christ, then you experience victory and effectiveness and can impart to others their sense of destiny and calling. You must find the place that God has for you and work there in partnership with others, both men and women. You must also be humble and discerning in your spirit lest you usurp an inheritance meant for others.

Each of us has a great responsibility to the generation that will follow us—our children. If they are to fully realize their place in God's plan, then we must give them a pure stream from which to drink—a stream unpolluted by bitterness, contention, division, unbelief, and fear; a stream where the way ahead has been cleared by pioneers and heroes who have gone before.

A Time for Heroes[*]

The Book of Nehemiah describes how the exiled Jews who returned to Jerusalem rebuilt the walls of the city and repaired many of the buildings. In the third chapter we find an interesting

---

[*] In August of 1998, Ministry to the Nations hosted its first "Women of Valor" Conference at Belmont Church in Nashville, Tennessee. The senior pastor of Belmont Church, Stephen Mansfield, is a man who firmly believes in women in ministry. In earlier years, he himself served as an associate pastor under a woman, and his wife, Trish, is one of the cell pastors of the church. There are several other women functioning within the church in leadership roles. Stephen is my pastor and dear friend who has spread his covering over me, urging me on to fulfill my calling in God. I honor him for his courage and leadership! The material in these next few sections is adapted from the message he gave at this conference. It was so good, and had such impact, that I wanted to include it in this book. I am deeply grateful for his allowing me to use it here.

reference: "Beyond him, Nehemiah son of Azbuk, ruler of a half-district of Beth Zur, made repairs up to a point opposite the tombs of David, as far as the artificial pool and the House of the Heroes" (Neh. 3:16 NIV). What was the "House of the Heroes"? According to historians, it was probably a barracks that had a special section set aside to honor the memories and exploits of the great heroes of the faith and of the Israelite nation. It probably contained artifacts or other memorabilia, such as scrolls, carvings, shields, swords, and the like.

The House of the Heroes was where the memory of the great ones was not only recalled, but also perpetuated and imparted to succeeding generations. An integral part of the restoration of Jerusalem and the returning of the people of God was the restoration of the House of the Heroes. These people recognized the importance of keeping alive the memories of the heroes of God.

Today there is a heroic anointing that God wants to place on His people. We have not been set free simply to celebrate our freedom; we have been set free for a purpose. God is restoring in this generation the heroic anointing of His male and female leaders to shape a generation that will walk in power.

A hero is someone who breaks through a barrier in one generation so that another people, another generation, can go even further. A hero is someone who lifts a canopy of oppression in one generation so that others can stand up under it.

For example, for centuries no man or woman on earth had ever broken the four-minute mile. In 1954 a British medical student by the name of Roger Bannister developed some new ways of training and broke the four-minute mile for the first time in history. You might think that a record that took so long to achieve would stand for a long time. However, less than two months later, someone else broke the four-minute mile. By the end of the year, 13 people had done it.

You Are Chosen!

Once someone proves that something can be done, it creates an environment of the possible, an impartation of hope and possibility that enables others to do it. It is a natural principle. The person who first breaks through the barrier makes it possible mentally and physically for others to break through. That's what being a hero means.

We have had many singular pioneers in past generations. What is different about today is that God has issued a call and is raising up thousands upon thousands of people like you and me to be the heroes and the pioneers for the generations that will follow us. It's great to be free in Christ, but if we celebrate that freedom for its own sake and hoard it for our own private benefit, then we will miss the ultimate calling that we have as heroes in our generation.

We are guardians of a deposit that God is pouring out on this generation. It's like the Niagara Falls—a great, thunderous flow of power and anointing that begins with us is meant to flow on to the next generation. How we walk today in our power and anointing will determine whether our children will inherit a pure or a polluted stream. If we do not cleanse our stream now, our impurities will be perpetuated and magnified in the next generation.

We live in an age that is sorely lacking in heroes. Think about it. Who can we look at today and regard as a hero? Certainly there are some, but they sure are hard to find! Isaiah the prophet said that when a people comes under judgment, God takes away wise leadership from the land—the hero, warrior, judge, prophet, elder, and others (see Is. 3:1-4 NIV). During a time of restoration the Lord restores these to the land. We are now entering such a time of restoration, and the Lord is calling us to be heroes. He is preparing us for a time soon to come when the world will cry out for leaders who are in touch with the heart and mind of God.

If you are going to accept your calling as a hero, you must be prepared to live vicariously. That is, you must be ready to live your life for the sake of others. That is just what Jesus did. His death on the cross for all our sins was a vicarious atonement—a substitutionary death on our behalf. True heroes don't perform for themselves or for personal gain, but for the good of others. They give themselves for the sake of another. That's what Joan of Arc did. That's what every truly great person does. Vicarious living is a truth that every true leader understands. God wants us to understand that we are to live today for the sake of our children and for a generation yet unborn. He has called us and anointed us to live heroically beyond the immediate and beyond the personal.

Keeping the Stream Pure

How can you be sure to maintain an unpolluted stream to pass on to those who follow? It requires hard work, a lot of prayer, and constant vigilance. There are seven general principles that we all need to take to heart that will help us keep our stream pure.

1. *Develop a passion for God's Word.* First Peter 3:15 says, "But in your hearts set apart Christ as Lord. Always be prepared to give an answer to everyone who asks you to give the reason for the hope that you have..." (NIV). Paul wrote to Timothy, "Do your best to present yourself to God as one approved, a workman who does not need to be ashamed and who correctly handles the word of truth" (2 Tim. 2:15 NIV). Being prepared to give an answer to those who ask about the hope we have requires more than just the testimony of our walk with God. It also requires knowledge of God's Word. Solid grounding in the Scriptures is needed if we hope to correctly handle the Word of truth.

How important is the Bible in your daily Christian life? Do you read it devotionally and let it go at that? Do you study it vigorously, trying to understand everything you can? Have you been hurt by the way others have used the Bible in the past to tie you down or hold you back and keep you from realizing God's call on your life? Because of this, have you distanced yourself from the Bible, telling yourself that you want to focus on being "spiritual" rather than biblical?

You Are Chosen!

If you are interested in accepting the anointing of a hero and living vicariously for another generation, understand that God is calling you to be *exactly* what Scripture teaches. None of us can afford to distance ourselves from Scripture, to settle for anything less than learning and understanding everything we can. For the sake of future generations we've got to hammer into the Scriptures and ask God for the understanding.

If you've left being biblical for the sake of being spiritual and pursuing your calling, come home. You don't have to neglect the Word to pursue your calling from God as a woman. The Word and the Spirit always agree. If the Holy Spirit is the One who both empowers you and releases you, then His Word is consistent with that. When you welcome a heroic anointing, when you welcome the call of God to be the heroic woman that you're called to be, then you welcome the responsibility to launch out on the firmest biblical foundation possible the generation that is rising.

2. *Expect to be wounded.* David the psalmist said to God, "For they persecute those You wound and talk about the pain of those You hurt" (Ps. 69:26 NIV). Have you ever been hurt because you were trying to stand up for Jesus? Do you carry deep pain over something that another person, even another Christian, said or did to you? Wounds are an occupational hazard for heroes. Whenever you accept the calling of God, whenever you stand up against the norm, you will be wounded. Wounds hurt. Sometimes they hurt very badly. Our theology of victory does not exempt us from bruises and wounds. God uses them to make us into the heroes that He has called us to be. Even if the wound comes from someone who is not in the Lord, the wound itself is something that God wants us to embrace redemptively.

Anything of value costs something. King David said that he would not offer to the Lord that which cost him nothing (see 2 Sam. 24:24). Everything we do as Christians takes on more meaning when we have paid a price for it. It's one thing to worship God on the good days when everything is going great. It's quite another thing to do so when we're under attack and hurting deep inside. Carrying the heroic anointing will cost us a price in hurt and pain. Many of you are already paying that price where you are. Take courage! The pain is worth the price if it means you can pass on an untainted stream to those who come after you. Embracing the pain for the sake of others is part of being a hero.

3. *God wounds you to develop your character.* To many people today, character means not doing certain things. That's not what it means in the Bible, however. In the Scriptures, the word *character* means to bear up under suffering and difficulty. In Ruth 3:11 (NIV), Ruth is called a woman of noble character because she bore up under difficulty.

God will use the hard things in your life to prepare you for the anointing that He wants to place upon you. The writer of Hebrews said of Jesus, "Although He was a son, He learned obedience from what He suffered" (Heb. 5:8 NIV). Think of what Jesus suffered: rejection by His family, the death of His earthly father, ridicule, crucifixion, and death. Through all this He learned obedience and thus became a source for His generation. In the same way the Lord uses the hardships of your life to build in you pillars of character that can sustain the anointing that will rest on them. God's anointing must work on you before it can work *through* you.

4. *Don't give place to bitterness.* Hebrews 12:15 says, "See to it that no one misses the grace of God and that no bitter root grows up to cause trouble and defile many" (NIV). The Greek word for "defile" carries the idea of a dye for coloring clothes. If you allow roots of bitterness to spring up in your life, they will dye or taint everything you do.

Have you ever heard someone speak where the words were great and the message solid, but there was something about his or her spirit that just didn't sit right with you? There may have been a root of bitterness or some other negative force that tainted the flow of their lives. Each of us as believers minister out of the flow of our spirits and out of the Holy Spirit in us. If we allow bitterness to dwell in our lives, we taint that flow and produce weakened, diseased fruit.

Anytime we take offense at a wrong or a hurt, we open ourselves up to be trapped by the enemy. The Greek word in the New Testament for "offense" is *skandalon*, from which we get the word *scandal*. It literally refers to a trap-stick or snare—that part of an animal trap that sets off the trap when the animal steps into it. Our bitterness, our offense, can become the trigger that snares us in the enemy's trap.

What do you do about bitterness in your life? When the Israelites in the wilderness complained to Moses because the water was too bitter to drink, Moses threw a piece of wood into the water and the water became sweet (see Ex. 15:23-25 NIV). When you throw the wood (the cross of Jesus) onto your waters of bitterness, they will become sweet.

5. *Submit to one another.* A lot of us get uncomfortable with the words *submit* or *submission,* and with good reason. There is no doubt that men have treated women wrongly throughout history. There's also no question that men often have acted as though they could go it alone without the gifts that women could bring. The great danger that lies in the current release of women into ministry is that it will degrade into a feministic Holy Spirit women's movement that is at odds with the men.

All of us, men and women, need to reexamine the Scriptures to understand the model that God intends. The apostle Paul summed up that model very nicely for the Ephesians: "Submit to one another out of reverence for Christ" (Eph. 5:21 NIV). What God wants now is not an independent women's movement and an independent men's movement, but a *teaming* that unfortunately most men and women in the Church don't yet understand. Submitting to one another out of reverence for Christ is the context for everything that follows. It's bad theology that has held women in bondage, not good theology. There is a place in certain contexts and situations for men to submit to women. There's a mutual deferring to gifts. There's a way women are created to carry certain things, and to do certain things, and a way men are created for certain things. If a man will love and protect his wife, if he will encourage her, she can be a tremendous fount of wisdom, revelation, and insight for him.

The quickest way to pollute the stream for the next generation is to make it an independent movement filled with harshness and unsubmissive spirits. God didn't intend the women to go it alone any more than He intended for the men to do so. He intended a godly merging. We can't afford to pass on to the next generation an ungodly spirit of independence.

6. *Don't compromise your call.* There is a tendency among Christian women today that when the traditional and normal corridors of power and ministry are closed to them, they seek alternative routes, especially the ones the men aren't interested in. Let's take intercession, for example. Frankly, most men aren't interested in intercession. There are many more women than men in the intercession ministry. Now, if that's your calling, get after it! Don't hesitate! But don't choose that route simply because it's a well-worn path for women—especially if your calling is somewhere else. You may be called to pastoral ministry or to evangelism. Don't let yourself be diverted. Don't compromise your call. The path of least resistance may *not* be the *right* path!

If you settle for what's easy or open to you right now, you may miss out on God's higher calling on your life. However, this doesn't mean engaging in guerrilla warfare either, blowing down doors and toppling walls in order to take your "rightful place"! We as women need to let the Lord be our defense and open those doors to us in His time and in His way. As we walk in the character we're called to walk in and as His anointing rests upon us, He will break those yokes. Don't compromise the high call in your heart. The Lord will prepare the way.

7. *Drive a stake in the heart of the fear of man.* Quite often the fear of man stems from the fact that we have too lofty a picture of humanity and too limited a picture of God. Man and his institutions seem so big and substantial while our concept of God is restrained by sin and unbelief. But as you grow in your walk with the Lord, as you learn to worship Him and behold His presence, as you cry out to Him, He will give you such a high view and a holy transforming vision of who Jesus is, and a high and transformed view of who you are and what you are called to be, that the opinions of men fade in comparison.

Chapter 40 of Isaiah has some powerful descriptions that compare mankind with God:

All men are like grass, and all their glory is like the flowers of the field. The grass withers and the flowers fall, because the breath of the Lord blows on them. Surely the people are grass. The grass withers and the flowers fall, but the word of our God stands forever....Surely the nations are like a drop in a bucket; they are regarded as dust on the scales; He weighs the islands as though they were fine dust....Before Him all the nations are as nothing; they are regarded by Him as worthless and less than nothing....He sits enthroned above the circle of the earth, and its people are like grasshoppers. He stretches out the heavens like a canopy, and spreads them out like a tent to live in. He brings princes to naught and reduces the rulers of this world to nothing. No sooner are they planted, no sooner are they sown, no sooner do they take root in the ground, than He blows on them and they wither, and a whirlwind sweeps them away like chaff....Do you not know? Have you not heard? The Lord is the everlasting God, the Creator of the ends of the earth. He will not grow tired or weary, and His understanding no one can fathom (Isaiah 40:6b-28 NIV).

How do you deal with the fear of man? Realize that the God who created the universe is the same God who has commissioned you. You are small, but He is BIG! He will strengthen and empower you in your adventure of faith.

Yes, exchange your fears. Cast off your fear of man and receive in its place the reverential fear of the Lord. Look at the Lord and see how awesome and omnipotent He is. Then look at yourself— you'll be overwhelmed by your smallness in contrast. But then take a look again—this BIG God is personally cheering you on. This everlasting God is on your side. As you understand this, the snare of the fear of man fades into the background and courage will rise up within you. Another piece is then put in place, and we all are ready to seize the day!

Carpe Diem—Seize the Day!

Take courage! You are chosen! The King of Heaven and earth has selected you to be His very own! He has called you to courage and to be a hero in this generation, living for the sake of the next. You are in good company. The Spirit of the Lord is with you, the same Spirit who led, inspired, and gave courage to Joan of Arc, Perpetua, Sojourner Truth, Harriet Tubman, Aimee Semple McPherson, Lydia Prince, Bertha Smith, Corrie ten Boom, Jackie Pullinger-To, and countless other women throughout the ages— women who heard God's call and seized the opportunity in their day. May we in this generation rise up and join this exalted company of the called, the chosen...His Beloved!

The following lines are from a song called "Hearts Courageous," written by Jamie Owens Collins and Dan Collins. May these words echo in our hearts and may they be our prayer to God:

A holy cloud of witnesses surrounds us as we war,
Saints and martyrs through the ages who have marched this way before,
And they cry, "O Church, take courage! It's Your time to take a stand—
Time to march with hearts courageous through the land."

In our hearts we hear the cadence of the drum.
The time to rise and face the enemy has come.
A time for hope, a time for courage, Knowing You will lead us through,
And we'll march with hearts courageous after You.

You Are Chosen!

Give us ears to hear that still small voice,
And give us lips forever willing to rejoice.
And may our eyes be lit with wisdom, May we know the path that's true,
And we'll march with hearts courageous after You.

We're marching on with hearts courageous.
We'll follow anywhere You want us to.
And should You lead us where the battle rages,
Let us march with hearts courageous after You.[1]

Let us enter the House of the Heroes. Let us look on the scrolls, carvings, shields, and swords. Let our eyes look into the faces and the hearts of heroes past. Let us lean forward, quiet in our souls, and listen for what advice and counsel they would give us. These stories of Joan of Arc, Perpetua, Harriet Tubman, and all the others are not just good "stories" or "legends." Their memorabilia is not just rotting cloth and rusting iron. Listen close and look deeply for what you can glean from them. They would say to you, "Serve the Lord with all your strength. Love Him with all your being! Do not miss the day of your visitation! While it is yet your day, seize it! Seize your destiny, your calling, your opportunity!" Seize the day!

Yes, there is a call to courage being pronounced in our day. Warriors are being sought for, searched for, and desperately needed. Do you hear the call? If so, then sign up right now!

Father, I surrender my life to the call to courage. Here I am. Change me. Use me. Drive fear out of me. I volunteer freely to be on the front lines in Jesus' name. Be glorified through my life. Amen!

Endnote

1. Jamie Owens Collins and Dan Collins, "Hearts Courageous," ©1985, and additional stanza and lyrics ©1994 by Fairhill Music. All Rights Reserved. International Copyright Secured. Used by permission.

JIM & MICHAL ANN GOLL

A CALL TO THE SECRET PLACE

A Call to the Secret Place is your personal invitation to take a step towards a place lovingly prepared for you by your Lord. Cheering you on will be the voices of other women who have discovered the Secret Place.
By Michal Ann Goll **$13.00**

THE LOST ART OF INTERCESSION

Restoring the Power and Passion of the Watch of the Lord

All over the globe God is moving—He is responding to the prayers of His people. Here Jim Goll teaches the lessons learned by the Moravians during their 100-year prayer Watch. They sent up prayers; God sent down His power. Through Scripture, the Moravian example, and his own prayer life, Jim Goll proves that "what goes up must come down."
By Jim Goll **$12.00**

KNEELING ON THE PROMISES

Birthing God's Purposes Through Prophetic Intercession

Covered in-depth are the many facets of prophetic intercession, including: travail—the prayer that births; four biblical definitions of intercession; listening, waiting, and watching; reminding God of His word; wisdom issues for intercessors; and promises for Israel and the Church.
By Jim Goll **$15.00**

TEACHING TAPES BY MICHAL ANN GOLL
2-Tape Albums, $10 Each

VISITATIONS IN THE NIGHT $10.00
WOMEN OF VALOR $10.00
A CALL TO THE SECRET PLACE $10.00
MESSAGES FROM THE MYSTICS $10.00
BLASTING THE ENEMY $10.00
HEAVENLY COMMUNICATIONS $10.00
INVADED BY THE SUPERNATURAL $10.00
UNMASKING UNGODLY BELIEFS $10.00

Visa, Mastercard, and checks are accepted.
A shipping and handling charge will be applied to your order.
Mail to: Ministry to the Nations, P.O. Box 1653, Franklin, TN 37065
FAX 615-599-5554   E-mail: info@mttnweb.com

WEBSITE: WWW.MICHALANNGOLL.COM

DEEP INSIDE EACH OF US IS A LONGING TO ESCAPE THE FRANTIC PACE OF LIFE IN THE TWENTY-FIRST CENTURY

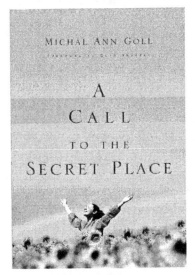

A CALL TO THE SECRET PLACE
BY MICHAL ANN GOLL

A Call to the Secret Place is your personal invitation to take that step towards the place lovingly prepared for you. Cheering you on will be the voices of other women as shared by Michal Ann Goll—women on the frontlines like Madam Guyon, Susanna Wesley, Fanny Crosby, Basilea Schlink, Gwen Shaw, Beth Alves and others. Their collective voices call out inviting you to join them in the privacy of a loving moment with your Lord.

ISBN 0-7684-2020-2

Also by Jim and Michal Ann Goll

INTERCESSION
by Jim W. Goll

The words of the intercessor are a power force for healing the wounds of the past and shaping the course of history. This book will help the intercessor release those words into the heavens and bring down God's will on earth. Goll shifts the focus of intercession away from the typical 'shot gun' approach of praying for the whole world in a single prayer.

ISBN 0-7684-2084-5

ELIJAH'S REVOLUTION
by Jim W. Goll and Lou Engle

A holy revolution of unprecedented dimension is underway today in America. In the face of relentless spiritual and moral decay, thousands of believers are answering God's call to a holy life of total and radical abandonment to Christ. Fired with the bold spirit of Elijah and the self giving heart of Esther, these latter day revolutionaries seek nothing less than the complete transformation of society through revival and spiritual awakening.

ISBN 0-7684-2057-1

WASTED ON JESUS
by Jim Goll

Wasted on Jesus defines a new generation of passionate lovers of the Lord Jesus. within the pages of this book you will be introduced to the hunger and passion of these 'wasted ones.' You will experience the collision of religion with reality, theology with thirst, and legalism with extravagant love.

ISBN 0-7684-2103-9

THE LOST ART OF INTERCESSION
by Jim Goll

When God's people send 'up' the incense of prayer and worship, God will send 'down' supernatural power, anointing, and acts of intervention. Jim Goll paints a picture of prophetic clarity and urgency in this anointed work that sounds God's clarion call to His Church: This is the season for us to mount the walls with prayer and praise-and restore The Lost Art of Intercession!

ISBN 1-56043-697-2

More titles from Destiny Image that you will enjoy reading

LADY IN WAITING
by Debby Jones and Jackie Kendall.
This is not just another book for single women! The authors, both well-known conference speakers, present an in-depth study on the biblical Ruth that reveals the characteristics every woman of God should develop. Learn how you can become a lady of faith, purity, contentment, patience—and much more—as you pursue a personal and intimate relationship with your Lord Jesus!
ISBN 1-56043-848-7
Devotional Journal and Study Guide
ISBN 1-56043-298-5

THE DELIGHT OF BEING HIS DAUGHTER
by Dotty Schmitt.
Discover the delight and joy that only being a daughter of God can bring! Dotty Schmitt's humorous and honest anecdotes of her own life and struggles in finding intimacy with God will encourage you in your own personal walk. Now in the pastoral and teaching ministry with her husband Charles at Immanuel's Church in the Washington, D.C. area, Dotty continues to experience and express the joy of following her Father.
ISBN 0-7684-2023-7

WOMAN: HER PURPOSE, POSITION, AND POWER
by Mary Jean Pidgeon.
When the enemy slipped into the garden, he robbed Eve and all her daughters of their original purpose, position, and power. But today God is bringing these truths back to their value in His Kingdom. Let Mary Jean Pidgeon, a wife, mother, and the Associate Pastor with her husband Pastor Jack Pidgeon in Houston, explain a woman's *purpose, position,* and *power.*
ISBN 1-56043-330-2

HINDS' FEET ON HIGH PLACES (Illustrated)
by Hannah Hurnard.
This illustrated version of the timeless classic was arranged by children's storyteller Dian Layton and beautifully illustrated by artist JoAnn Edington. It tells the story of Much-Afraid and her journey to the High Places with the Shepherd. Filled with exciting adventure and a triumphant conclusion, this story will teach your child the importance of following the Shepherd.
ISBN 0-7684-2021-0

Additional copies of this book and other
book titles from DESTINY IMAGE are
available at your local bookstore.

For a bookstore near you, call 1-800-722-6774

Send a request for a catalog to:

Destiny Image ® Publishers, Inc.
P.O. Box 310
Shippensburg, PA 17257-0310

*"Speaking to the Purposes of God for This
Generation and for the Generations to Come"*

**For a complete list of our titles,
visit us at www.destinyimage.com**